BOOKS BY W. S. MERWIN

POEMS

The First Four Books of Poems (INCLUDING *A Mask for Janus,
The Dancing Bears, Green with Beasts and
The Drunk in the Furnace*)   *1975*
Writings to an Unfinished Accompaniment   *1973*
The Carrier of Ladders   *1970*
The Lice   *1967*
The Moving Target   *1963*
The Drunk in the Furnace   *1960*
Green with Beasts   *1956*
The Dancing Bears   *1954*
A Mask for Janus   *1952*

PROSE

The Miner's Pale Children   *1970*

TRANSLATIONS

Osip Mandelstam, Selected Poems (with Clarence Brown)   *1974*
Asian Figures   *1973*
Transparence of the World (Poems by Jean Follain)   *1969*
Voices (Poems by Antonio Porchia)   *1969*
Products of the Perfected Civilization (Selected Writings
of Chamfort)   *1969*
Twenty Poems of Love and a Song of Despair (Pablo Neruda) *1969*
Selected Translations 1948–1968   *1968*
The Song of Roland   *1963*
Lazarillo de Tormes   *1962*
The Satires of Persius   *1961*
Spanish Ballads   *1960*
The Poem of the Cid   *1959*

W. S. MERWIN

The First Four
Books of Poems

W.S.MERWIN

The First Four Books of Poems

A Mask for Janus
The Dancing Bears
Green with Beasts
The Drunk in the Furnace

ATHENEUM   *NEW YORK*

1975

The books collected in this volume were originally published as follows:

A Mask for Janus: Yale University Press, New Haven, 1952
The Dancing Bears: Yale University Press, New Haven, 1954
Green with Beasts: Alfred A. Knopf, New York, 1956
The Drunk in the Furnace: The Macmillan Company, New York, 1960

A Mask for Janus: copyright © 1952 by Yale University Press
The Dancing Bears: copyright © 1954 by Yale University Press
Green with Beasts: copyright © 1955, 1956 by W. S. Merwin
The Drunk in the Furnace: copyright © 1956, 1957, 1958, 1959, 1960
by W. S. Merwin

Library of Congress catalog card number 75-4079
ISBN 0-689-10668-8
Published simultaneously in Canada by McClelland and Stewart Ltd.
Manufactured by Halliday Lithograph Corporation,
West Hanover and Plympton, Massachusetts
First Edition

AUTHOR'S NOTE

These poems are reprinted exactly as they appeared in the four books in which they were originally published. They have not been revised, rearranged, or altered for better or worse.

CONTENTS

A MASK FOR JANUS

THE DANCING BEARS

GREEN WITH BEASTS

Part One: Physiologus

Part Two

Part Three

THE DRUNK IN THE FURNACE

A Mask for Janus

(1952)

FOR DOROTHY

Habit is evil, all habit, even speech
And promises prefigure their own breech.

JOHN WHEELWRIGHT

. . . pone cara de mia . . .

PEDRO SALINAS

ANABASIS (I)

Then we poised, in time's fullness brought
As to a new country, the senses
In the mutations of a sallow light,
A season signs and speechless;

Thought momently on nothing, knew
No oratory, no welcome:
Silence about our silence grew;
Beached by the convenient stream.

Night is familiar when it comes.
On dim gestures does the mind
Exorcise abandoned limbs,
Disbodied, of that other land

Estranged almost beyond response,
A bleached and faintly relevant
Signature to sir the sense
In veteran usage and intent.

One dreams fixed beasts that drowse or wonder,
Not blinking; by the stream a few
Poplars and white beeches where
Exhausted leaves, suspended, through

The distant autumn do not fall,
Or, fallen, fired, are unconsumed,
The flame perduring, the still
Smoke eternal in the mind.

3

(Embarrassed, these scarred penates
Smile, between raw stones supported,
Musing perhaps an anomalous
Speech no longer understood.)

We ponder, after damp sundown,
The slow boats departing, heavy,
In another time; our direction
Moved in the cool rain away:

We with brief knowledge hazarded
Alien influence and tropic,
Entered and did diversely thread
What degradations, false music,

Straits whose rocks lean to the sound,
Monstrous, of their declivites,
As lovers on their private ground
See no distance, but face and face;

We have passed in a warm light
Islands whose charmed habitants
Doze on the shores to dissipate
The seasons of their indolence;

Even against those borders led
Lapped by the forgetful rivers
Have stood among the actual dead,
No breath moving the gray flowers.

The remnant of all passage lies
Cold or distorted in the brain
As tall fables of strangers, as
Lisped visions of other men.

(The neighbor waters flame and wave:
All that we could not bring away
Our hands, as though with courage, have
Burned, and the tired ships where they lay.)

The covenant we could but seize
Fractionally by the ear
And dreamed it substance, that the eyes
Might follow—and its motions were

Hands that toy about a door
In dreams and melt where they caress,
Not displacing the wind they wear—
Brought us to this final place.

We see the various brain enclosed
Never the promise, but its guise:
Terrain in private we supposed
That always in its Easter is.

Rather, in priestly winter bide
Our shadows where no prayers will work
That unison we faintly, toward
Our time and litany, invoke.

You, satisfied under no sky,
Even from this air your air is fled,
Your singular authority
Vain, no richness where you bled,

But you are dwindled and now die
To a vexed but promissory shape
For an old man stroked always by
The vague extremities of sleep:

So were he tangled to believe,
By euphory and the leaves' dictions.
His grave members did walk and weave,
Blessed, among the many mansions.

ANABASIS (II)

After the first night and bare morning passed
We remembered the gray wings of a gull
That traced us seaward when our eyes had lost
The thread of last whiteness where the land fell.

After the first days, one when the world turned
Dark and the rain came, we remembered fires
In lost houses; we stared and lurched half-blind
Against new darkness, neither night's nor ours.

We survived the selves that we remembered;
We have dozed on gradual seas where slowly
The hours changed on the silence, and a word,
Falling, expired in the sufficient day.

Sometimes through a mirage or evening rose
Towers where the myths sleep and the lanterns;
We fled a saeculum what sick repose,
But woke at morning where the fever burned.

We have slid on a seizure of the wind
To spume-blindness where our fear became
A whirling without chronicle or end;
There we circled and bent the thought of time

Till, saved by violence from violence,
We, the gesture of rages not our own,
Forsook and followed, motion without sense,
Where we were drawn, from pool and tempest thrown.

In wake of storms we came where the gulls cry
Allusions to dim archipelagoes;
We coaxed our souls and sembled where we lay
The last exhaustion, as the buzzard knows.

We had seen strengths flee or degenerate:
Even the wind starved in our tracks and died,
Till, on that mirror, we, the image, thought,
After the petrel-, of the halcyon-dead.

Thus calmed we lay and hungered east or west
But drifted on what warm meridian,
Grazing the reefs of dying; yet we passed
Through that peripety and afternoon.

We saw the islands of a new season.
We were made young with watching, and our eyes
Believed a garden and reserve where swung
The fruits that from all hungers immunize.

There when we called, the startled land returned
A precipitate waking as of a child;
Our vision built on the approaching sand;
We entered channels where the coral smiled,

And but the countries of occasion found:
There at sundown, lodged where the tide lingers,
Among the driftwood and the casual drowned,
Slept on the lulled questions of those rivers.

We have half-waked to hear the minutes die
And heard our minds that, waiting toward the east,
Embraced the seed and thought of day, and we
Were by the pool of dark the crouchèd beast.

But not the watchers of unheard-of shores
Know to repeat our prayers when we became
The eyes of sleep that chased receding fires
Through the bodiless exile of a dream.

Between sleep and the vacant excellence
Of seas we suffered music that declares
The monstrous fixities of innocence;
We are children of a different curse.

In dream there was no answer nor command,
Yet there did rumors beyond reason sway
Waters that slipped from an escaping land
All night, and we are tidal and obey.

We were already far when morning died.
We watched the colors sink, and all the light.
We turned from silence and fearfully made
Our small language in the place of night.

In fear of the swift bird that shouts and sees
In these tides and dark entrails the curled
Augurs of unreasonable seas
We seek a new dimension for the world.

But sentenced are the seasons that we know.
The serpent holds and the whirlwind harries
The last oceans where the drowned pursue
The daze and fall of fabulous voyages.

Still we are strange to orisons and knees.
Fixed to bone only, foreign as we came,
We float leeward till mind and body lose
The uncertain continent of a name.

RIME OF THE PALMERS

Where, and in the morning,
Palmers, do you pass?
The sudden birds sing
In the poplar trees.

Where, and away from morning,
Palmers, do you follow,
And where are you going
That you take no shadow,

And what carry, stranger,
That no shadow take?
—Hunger is sleeping where
Staff and shadow break.

Bone and vein are full
Where we sat at meat;
We seek the still
Wonder that we eat.

Our motion is our form
And our passage raiment;
Between stillness and time
We pass, improvident.

—Form is a thing goes slyly
And escapes our ears;
In another country
What did you love, palmers,

And what do you remember
This morning and light?
—We go (may wonder
Send and receive our feet)

Half-remembering
Where our bones were hid
And the wind at evening
There where hunger died,

And the evening wind
That everywhere and sorely
Turned and complained
As we came away.

—The wind is at morning
On the high meadow;
What are you singing,
Palmers, as you go,

And what do your lips say
When I hear no sounds?
—Speech is a thorny way
In a hard land,

And into absence,
Into quiet goes:
Before the silence,
After the voice,

We sing, and without words,
An air of promise,
As the waking birds
In the poplar trees.

—The last stars show
On the chill season;
You start betimes, you go,
Palmers, in night and dawn:

You move to what increase,
Neither night's nor day's?
—The winds disposing peace
Their where our vision is;

But, moving, shall we say
We are fire or storm,
Or as one that, wholly
Name, or without a name,

Comes, or has appeared,
Or the voice thereafter?
Who knows the word
That we are carol for?

A word is a little thing,
And the letter kills,
And you are far who sing
From the morning hills,

And what is the high road,
And the road where you go?
—We have been the dead
And what the dead know:

At the broken bridge
Where the cold rivers
Move in a rage,
Let the breath be prayers;

If music speak softly
Forget what it tells
Where you go blind and high
By the wild hills;

At the nighted gates
By the last mountain
There age forgets
And the child is slain:

If hope bring you there
Where night's self darkly burns,
Abandon hope to air
And to the wind's returns;

If a dim leaf tremble
And then the dawn come back,
Oh, begin carols
By that morning lake.

—But pleasure discovers
By what sense and lights,
Bridge and hills, palmers,
And the nighted gates?

But you leave us. Afterward
What shall we say, palmers?
Say: the birds suddenly
Sing in the poplar trees.

That the word was morning once
That is common day;
In mention of our bones,
Of our bodies say:

Rain is a perilous friend,
The sweet wind blows foreign;
These pictures made of mind
And these hungers gone

And these palmers that on
A field of summer went
Are perfect and lie down
Thus, lest the land repent.

BALLAD OF JOHN CABLE
AND THREE GENTLEMEN

He that had come that morning,
One after the other,
Over seven hills,
Each of a new color,

Came now by the last tree,
By the red-colored valley,
To a gray river
Wide as the sea.

There at the shingle
A listing wherry
Awash with dark water;
What should it carry?

There on the shelving,
Three dark gentlemen.
Might they direct him?
Three gentlemen.

"Cable, friend John, John Cable,"
When they saw him they said,
"Come and be company
As far as the far side."

"Come follow the feet," they said,
"Of your family,
Of your old father
That came already this way."

But Cable said, "First I must go
Once to my sister again;
What will she do come spring
And no man on her garden?

She will say "Weeds are alive
From here to the Stream of Friday;
I grieve for my brother's plowing,'
Then break and cry."

"Lose no sleep," they said, "for that fallow:
She will say before summer,
'I can get me a daylong man,
Do better than a brother.' "

Cable said, "I think of my wife:
Dearly she needs consoling;
I must go back for a little
For fear she die of grieving."

"Cable," they said, "John Cable,
Ask no such wild favor;
Still, if you fear she die soon,
The boat might wait for her."

But Cable said, "I remember:
Out of charity let me
Go shore up my poorly mother,
Cries all afternoon."

They said, "She is old and far,
Far and rheumy with years,
And, if you like, we shall take
No note of her tears."

But Cable said, "I am neither
Your hire man nor maid,
Your dog nor shadow
Nor your ape to be led."

He said, "I must go back:
Once I heard someone say
That the hollow Stream of Friday
Is a rank place to lie;

And this word, now I remember,
Makes me sorry: have you
Thought of my own body
I was always good to?

The frame that was my devotion
And my blessing was,
The straight bole whose limbs
Were long as stories—

Now, poor thing, left in the dirt
By the Stream of Friday
Might not remember me
Half tenderly."

They let him nurse no worry;
They said, "We give you our word:
Poor thing is made of patience;
Will not say a word."

"Cable, friend John, John Cable,"
After this they said,
"Come with no company
To the far side.

To a populous place,
A dense city
That shall not be changed
Before much sorrow dry."

Over shaking water
Toward the feet of his father,
Leaving the hills' color
And his poorly mother

And his wife at grieving
And his sister's fallow
And his body lying
In the rank hollow,

Now Cable is carried
On the dark river;
Nor even a shadow
Followed him over.

On the wide river
Gray as the sea
Flags of white water
Are his company.

MENG TZU'S SONG

The sparrows gleaning gutters
Kick and shuffle the horsehair,
And the simple wind that stirs
Their feathers stirs my hair.

How can I know, now forty
Years have shuffled my shoulders,
Whether my mind is steady
Or quakes as the wind stirs?

Because one sparrow, running
On the old wind-ruts, can be
Turned by an unseen thing,
A small wind in the sky,

And changes, it sets me thinking;
Yet I know not if my mind
Is moved, or is but sinking
Alone to its own kind.

If my mind moves not in wind
Or other breaths, it is not
Strange; at forty the mind
Of Kao Tzu wavered not.

Lo, how is the kept wind let
Out to make trouble with me!
How can one remain not
Moving before his eye?

One cultivates bravery
That the skin's hair not flinch
Nor the frail eye flee
Nor the blood blanch.

One is as the trodden inch
Of horsehair on the bare ground
At the market place: wrench
Nor kick wring from him sound.

Thinks he as though he were sand
Or horsehair, should the stiff sword
Shave the strength from his mind
And stab away his word.

Thinks of defeat and blood,
All hairs blown from control,
The hands like hair in mud
As though it mattered little.

How can the thin mind be able?
How put off quaking only,
Keeping all else simple,
Even in wind steady?

The wind is stiff and is high.
Simple the wind. The open
Coat of horsehair on three
Sides flaps without passion.

BLIND WILIAM'S SONG

Stand from my shadow where it goes
Threaded upon a white dream,
From my clear eyes that take no light
And give no mercy.

I stood in clean Monday and heard
Seventy tongues of fire
Burn down from their talk.
I am the ash that walk.

Tuesday was dusty feet;
I shall not be the first
Who walked and did not know
The earth, the middle earth.

Wednesday, if it came,
I was a blown curse
And who are you not withered?
Tempt not my memory.

But though I was, on Thursday,
In that late morning,
Multiple as rain
And fell as rain falls

And have been on Friday
Say a white horse racing
—Since I see no motion
All speed is easy—

I have not been the sea
(My dry bone forbids me)
Whose blind repeated loss
Any loud tide will serve.

Lull the stones over me,
I that on Saturday
Closed about myself
And raged and was the grave.

Sunday I lie down
Within without my body;
All colored creation
Is tamed white by time.

FOR A DISSOLVING MUSIC

What shall be seen?
Limbs of a man
old and alone,
his shadow with him,
going and gone.
What shall be heard?
A hollow rime:
the heart gone tame
knocking afraid.
What shall be known?
Briefly the name,
but its frame shaken,
house of time
blown and broken,
draughty room,
dwindled flame,
red coal come
out of the warm,
dry honeycomb,
ended dream.

What shall be said?
This word if any:
time and blood
are spent money,
rain in a sieve;
summer is dead
(whom fools believe)
in a far grave,
worms receive

her fire to wive,
fear walks alive,
prayers I would weave,
pains I have,
hopes not many;
wherefore grieve
o splintered stave,
withered glove,
dry groove,
shaken sleeve
empty of love.

What shall be sung?
This song uneven:
eleven, seven,
chance cloven,
joints spavin,
blood chill-driven,
flesh craven,
breath not often,
teeth riven,
all day shriven,
last coven,
all night raven,
all doom woven,
none forgiven,
no curse ungraven,
no peace at even,
remnant for leaven,
promise true-given,
field but shaven,
nor hope of heaven.

HALF ROUNDEL

I make no prayer
For the spoilt season,
The weed of Eden.
I make no prayer.
     Save us the green
     In the weed of time,

Now is November;
In night uneasy
Nothing I say.
I make no prayer.
     Save us from water
     That washes us away.

What I do ponder?
All smiled disguise,
Lights in cold places.
I make no prayer.
     Save us from air
     That wears us loosely.

The leaf of summer
To cold has come
In little time.
I make no prayer.
     From earth deliver
     And the dark therein.

Now is no whisper
Through all the living.
I speak to nothing.
I make no prayer.
  Save use from fire
  Consuming up and down.

A DANCE OF DEATH

King

I saw from a silk pillow
All high stations and low
Smile when I spoke, and bow,
And obey and follow.
All men do as I do.
I went in gold and yellow,
Ermine and gemmed shoe,
And was human even so,
Et, ecce, nunc in pulvere dormio.

Monk

I hoped that all sinners who
Wore a saintly sorrow
Into heaven should go.
All this did I do:
Walk with the eyes low,
Keep lonely pillow,
Many days go
Fasting and hollow,
All my bounty bestow,
Et, ecce, nunc in pulvere dormio.

Scholar

I sat like a shadow,
The light sallow,
Reasoning yes and no.
One thing I came to know.
I heard the mouse go,
Heard whispers in the tallow,
Wind disputing, "Although . . ."
Night on the candle blow,
Et, ecce, nunc in pulvere dormio.

Huntsman

The wind blew
In the cold furrow;
The falcon flew;
These did I follow:
Deerhound, doe,
Fox upon snow,
And sent the arrow,
And was chased, who did follow,
And came to this burrow,
Et, ecce, nunc in pulvere dormio.

Farmer

I walked with plow
On the green fallow;
All I did harrow
Dirt does undo.
Out at elbow
I lie to mellow,
Set in a furrow,

The weeds' fellow,
Quod, ecce, nunc in pulvere dormio.

Woman

I was as green willow,
My hands white and slow,
Love and increase below.
Be reaped as you did sow.
I am bitter as rue.
Now am I also
Defaced and hollow,
Nursing no shadow,
Quod, ecce, nunc in pulvere dormio.

Epitaph

Lords, I forget what I knew;
I saw false and true,
Sad and antic show,
Did profane and hallow,
Saw the worthies go
Into the still hollow
And wrote their words, even so,
Et, ecce, nunc in pulvere dormio.

VARIATION ON A LINE BY EMERSON

In May, when sea-winds pierced our solitudes,
In the May winds not yet warmed out of malice,
At a certain doorway once I stood, my face
Leaning westward, a little before evening—
Oh, though all breath be seasonal, who can tell
A story like new grass blown in sunlight?

In May when winds blow westward into the light
As though both would depart our solitudes,
Though the door be different, what can I tell,
Feeling the sun thus fail from all life and malice?
But once the measure and sight of day, at evening,
Died in the shadows, so, of a cold face.

You that have forsaken the door, the face,
Burgeon, body, decrease, the turning light,
Who keep such single quiet both morning and evening
That approach but multiplies your solitudes,
Whether the bodily death is death to malice
Not the intrusions of sea-wind tell.

Let a kind diction out of the shadows tell,
Now toward my slumber, a legend unto my face
Of sleep as a quiet garden without malice
Where body moves, after the bitter light,
A staid dance among innocent solitudes;
So let me lie in a story, heavy with evening.

But I dream of distances where at evening
Ghost begins (as no migrant birds can tell)

A journey through outlandish solitudes,
Hair all ways lifted, leaves wild against face,
Feet trammeled among dune grass, with spent light,
And finds no roof at last against wind or malice.

Sir, who have locked your doors, but without malice,
Or madam, who draw your shawl against evening,
By the adumbrations of your thin light
What but this poor contention can you tell:
Ceaseless intruders have demeaned your face
And contrived homesteads in your solitudes.

Tell me who keeps infrangible solitudes
But the evening's dead on whose decided face
Morning repeats the malice and the light.

OVER THE BIER OF THE WORLDING

My friends, what can I say,
Having forgotten the feeling and the time
When it seemed that a dull body,
That even a dead man could dream
Those small belligerent birds, perhaps one gull,
Turning over the foul
Pond by the colliery,
These waters flicked by a regardless wind,
And the clouds, not of this country,
Sailing, as I had imagined;
Then these faces, even as I am, stilled,
Conforming to the world.
That which I kept, one body
And a few clothes, are brought to following
Processes as of poverty,
Suffering but not knowing,
Lying unimproved by the long season
And the falling rain.

EPITAPH ON CERTAIN SCHISMATICS

These were they whom the body could not please,
Shaded between the shaded lights who rose
Quavering and forsook the arrogant knees,
The bodies death had made incredulous.
They had known, that season, lights in the trees
Moving when none felt wind, whisper of candles,
Pursuit of strange hinds, signs in snarled spindles,
Omens from alien birds, and after these
They descended into Hell. "Suffering is
Measure of nothing, now measure is lost," one said.
They fell to stroking their shyest histories.
Even cool flesh (so gaunt they grew and loveless),
When they could best remember it, only made
A wry shadow between the quick and the dead.

SUSPICOR SPECULUM

To Sisyphus

Seeing, where the rock falls blind, this figure
At whispers swaying the drained countenance,
As might a shadow stand, I have stayed an hour
To no sound but his persistent sibilance,
Aghast, as should the populous dreaming head
See evils colder than the brain yet burn,
Or swift and tomorrow the enormous dead
Scatter their pose and, Sisyphus, return.
Patience betrays and the time speaks nothing. Come,
Pursed in the indigent small dark confess:
Is mine this shade that to all hours the same
Lurches and fails, marine and garrulous—
A vain myth in the winter of his sense,
Capable neither of song nor silence?

EPITAPH

Death is not information.
Stone that I am,
He came into my quiet
And I shall be still for him.

ODE: THE MEDUSA FACE

When did I pass the pole where I deprived
Three hags of their one eye, then, staring, seized
The total of their dark
And took their answer?
For that way I came though the eye forgets:
Now tall over the breathless shore this day
Lifts on one equal glare
The crass and curling face.
I cannot tell if stone is upon me
Healing me, clotting time until I stand
Dead. If the heart yet moves,
What shield were faithful found,
What weapon? I stand as in sloth of stone,
Amazed, for a maimed piece of one's own death,
Should that lithe hair stiffen,
Were the shape of her fall.

FESTIVAL

Laughter is not celebration
And may not coax with renewal
The closed heads bending
In their garden at heal of evening.

I that am king of no country—
Shall a mind of dry leaves
On the erstwhile meadow
Invoke for me a gray retinue?

I would have a weather
Of spells and reflections
Whether dawn or a moon hang
In the green lagoon where fish swim.

You have seen the afternoon
Turn among shadows under
A flutter of paper and laurel.
Was that a dance or hesitancy?

And a body that made
A spectre his companion,
Fruitless until dark,
Lay down and embraced a lean shadow.

DICTUM: FOR A MASQUE OF DELUGE

for Dido

There will be the cough before the silence, then
Expectation; and the hush of portent
Must be welcomed by a diffident music
Lisping and dividing its renewals;
Shadows will lengthen and sway, and, casually
As in a latitude of diversion
Where growth is topiary, and the relaxed horizons
Are accustomed to the trespass of surprise,
One with a mask of Ignorance will appear
Musing on the wind's strange pregnancy.

And to him one must enter from the south
In a feigned haste, with disaster on his lips,
And tales of distended seas, continents
Submerged, worlds drowned, and of drownings
In mirrors; unto this foreboding
Let them add sidelong but increasing mention,
With darkening syllables, of shadows, as though
They stood and traded restlessness beneath
A gathering dark, until their figures seem
But a flutter of speech down an expense of wind.

So, with talk, like a blather of rain, begun,
Weather will break and the artful world will rush
Incontinent. There must be a vessel.
There must be rummage and shuffling for salvation
Till on that stage and violence, among
Curtains of tempest and shaking sea,
A covered basket, where a child might lie,
Timbered with osiers and floated on a shadow,

Glides adrift, as improbably sailing
As a lotus flower bearing a bull.

Hills are to be forgotten; the patter of speech
Must lilt upon flatness. The beasts will come;
And as they come, let one man, by the ark,
Drunken with desolation, his tongue
Rounding the full statement of the seasons,
Tremble and stare, his eyes seeming to chase
A final clatter of doomed crows, to seek
An affirmation, a mercy, an island,
Or hills crested with towns, and to find only
Cities of cloud already crumbling.

And these the beasts: the bull from the lotus flower
With wings at his shoulders; and a goat, winged;
A serpent undulating in the air;
A lion with wings like falling leaves;
These are to wheel on a winged wheel above
The sullen ark, while hare, swine, crocodile,
Camel and mouse come; and the sole man, always,
Lurches on childish limbs above the basket—
To his mere humanity seas shall not attain
With tempest, nor the obscure sky with torches.

(Why is it rumored that these beasts come in pairs
When the anatomies of their existence
Are wrought for singularity? They walk
Beside their shadows; their best motions are
Figments on the drapery of the air.
Their propagation is a redoubling
Merely of dark against the wall, a planetary
Leaning in the night unto their shadows

And stiffening to the moment of eclipse;
Shadows will be their lean progeny.)

At last the sigh of recession: the land
Wells from the water; the beasts depart; the man
Whose shocked speech must conjure a landscape
As of some country where the dead years keep
A circle of silence, a drying vista of ruin,
Musters himself, rises, and stumbling after
The dwindling beasts, under the all-colored
Paper rainbow, whose arc he sees as promise,
Moves in an amazement of resurrection,
Solitary, impoverished, renewed.

A falling frond may seem all trees. If so
We know the tone of falling. We shall find
Dictions for rising, words for departure;
And time will be sufficient before that revel
To teach an order and rehearse the days
Till the days are accomplished: so now the dove
Makes assignations with the olive tree,
Slurs with her voice the gestures of the time:
The day foundering, the dropping sun
Heavy, the wind a low portent of rain.

THE BONES OF PALINURUS PRAY TO THE
NORTH STAR

Console us. The wind chooses among us.
Our whiteness is a night wake disordered.
Lone candor, be constant over
Us desolate who gleam no direction.

SESTINA

for Robert Graves

Where I came by torchlight there is dawn-song:
Leaves remembering, sudden as a name
Recalled from nowhere, remembering morning,
Fresh wind in high grass, cricket on plowshare,
Whisper of stream in the green-shadowed place,
Thrush and tanager keeping season.

Have I not also willed to be heard in season?
Have I not heard anger raised in a song
And watched when many went out to a wild place
And fought with the dark to make themselves a name?
I have seen of those champions how thin a share
After one night shook off their sleep at morning.

In a stony month a long cloud darkened morning.
Their feet gone white, shuffling the cold season,
The breath of some was worn too small to share.
Have I not heard how fragile then grew song?
Gray water lashed at the island of one's name.
And some stayed to flutter empty in that place.

What road is it one follows out of that place?
I remember no direction. I dreamed of morning,
Walking, warming the tongue over a name.
And a few of us came out of that season
As though from sleep, and stood too bleak for song,
And saw hills and heaven in the one dawn share.

Whom shall I praise before the gray knife share?
I have gone like seed into a dark place.

Whom shall I choose to make new with song?
For there will be sinking between night and morning,
Lisp of hushed voices, a dwindled season,
The small lights that flicker at a name.

Where again shall I walk with various name?
Merciless restlessness falls to my share.
Whose house shall I fill for more than a season?
I woke with new words, and in every place,
Under different lights, evening and morning,
Under many masters studied one song.

A breathed name I was with no resting-place,
A bough of sleep that had no share of morning,
Till I had made body and season from a song.

HERONS

As I was dreaming between hills
That stones wake in a changing land,
There in the country of morning
I slept, and the hour and shadow slept.

I became the quiet stone
By a river where the winds
Favor honest thoughts. Three herons
Rose into a hemlock tree.

And I heard, "All day I stand
Dreaming that the night has come;
Beneath my wings, beneath my feet
The resignation and the death."

And, "When will darkness bury me
Who stand all day with open eye,
The small eye through which the years pass
From one place to another place."

And, "I have neither eye nor dream;
Dumb as with sleep or dignity
I stand, and others speak of me
In questions, but no prophecy."

But I knew neither dream nor eye
And held my question till a wind
Shook them in their hemlock tree
And I became the man who fell

After the lightning long ago
At his own window; there he stood
And leaned out on the afternoon
Till someone touched him, and he fell.

Daylong I dreamed as one who sets
His impudence in a falling house
And laughs and sleeps. The ruined hour
Moves and outmodes this comedy.

Who will see me if I fall?
I waked between the quiet hills;
I saw the dark and came away
And night where I had lain all day.

SONG WITH THE EYES CLOSED

I am the shape in sleep
While the seasonal beasts
With petulant rough step
Forsake my random coasts.

I am the face recedes
Though the pool be constant
Whose double kingdom feeds
The sole vein's discontent.

I have seen desire, such
As a violent hand,
Murder my sleep—as much
Is suffered of the wind.

CANCIÓN Y GLOSA

*Y yo, mientras, hijo
tuyo, con mas secas
hojas en las venas.*

Jiménez

Among the almond trees
whiteness more than winter's,
speech where no name is,
flowers broken from sleep;
and you their litany,
a breath upon this fervor,
you their reason, lady,
seem as a name, meanwhile,
for an immortal season,
who stand in such whiteness
with these green leaves in your hands.

There is no breath of days
in that time where I was,
in that place, through the trees;
no winds nor satellites,
seasons nor bodies rise;
are no descent of rivers,
wavering of fishes,
indecision of tides,
langor before pause,
nor any dance to please,
nor prayers, pleasure of knees,
coupling, smile of increase,

swaying of fruit and seas,
genesis, exodus,
tremor of arteries,
decay by calendars,
hum of carrion flies;
and no shadow-plays,
trepidation of fingers,
ruse of limbs or faces
ghosts nor histories
shift before the eyes,
but that vain country lies
in savorless repose.

    Among the names of these,
yet as the eyes remove
now from the polities
of these disstated things,
I their artifice,
a breath among such langor,
I their name, lady,
seem as one nameless, leaning
through such stillness meanwhile
with these dry leaves in my hands.

CAROL

On vague hills the prophet bird
Chants now the night is drained;
What was the stem this night stirred
And root from the winter ground?

Lord, Lord, and no night remained,
But heaven only, whence comes
Light such as no sun contained,
And the earth shook, and our limbs.

By song we were brought to stand
By that flower where frail our eyes
Strayed among beasts and found
Dim kings dreaming on their knees.

Lord, Lord, and earth's hours were torn
To dreams and we beheld there
On that silence newly born
Heaven's light in the still flower.

From such a quiet wakened,
After the vision has burned
On such birth, to what end
Have dew and hours returned?

Lord, Lord, and what remember
We of dreams when the day comes,
And the loud bird laughs on wonder
And white sheep lying like tombs?

We who are flesh have no word
And distraction is our music,
Who on the anxious night heard
Peace over our voices break.

CAROL OF THE THREE KINGS

How long ago we dreamed
Evening and the human
Step in the quiet groves
And the prayer we said:
Walk upon the darkness,
Words of the lord,
Contain the night, the dead
And here comfort us.
We have been a shadow
Many nights moving,
Swaying many nights
Between yes and no.
We have been blindness
Between sun and moon
Coaxing the time
For a doubtful star.
Now we cease, we forget
Our reasons, our city,
The sun, the perplexed day,
Noon, the irksome labor,
The flushed dream, the way,
Even the dark beasts,
Even our shadows.
In this night and day
All gifts are nothing:
What is frankincense
Where all sweetness is?
We that were followers
In the night's confusion
Kneel and forget our feet

Who the cold way came.
Now in the darkness
After the deep song
Walk among the branches
Angels of the lord,
Over earth and child
Quiet the boughs.
Now shall we sing or pray?
Where has the night gone?
Who remembers day?
We are breath and human
And awake have seen
All birth and burial
Merge and fall away,
Seen heaven that extends
To comfort all the night,
We have felt morning move
The grove of a few hands.

CAROL

Lady, the dew of years
Makes sodden the world
And yet there is no morning.
Lady, we cannot think you
Indifferent or far,
And we lean and call after
You who in the night,
As a morning, among
This our heaviness came
And our eyes called you maiden.
We are in the darkness,
Our eyes turned to the door,
Waiting. Because you passed
Through the room where we are,
Your form not cumbered
With our weight and gesture;
Waiting, because you went
Uncontained by our shadows,
As a light, quietly;
Leaning, as though you might
Come again where our eyes
Are lost that follow after
You who as a light
Through the room where we are
With grace carried a flower.

A POEM FOR DOROTHY

No shape in darkness single stands
And we in privacy and night,
Taking surprise of love for light,
Merged the dark fortunes of our hands.

Patience of fire insists and warms
Through dust, through dusty bone the breath;
The car and intellect of death
Direct of love the heated forms.

Sitting on stones we kiss to please
Some stilled remembrance that shares our blood,
And warmth whose shape and name were dead
From ruin moving amends our peace.

HERMIONE ON SIMULACRA

for Diana Wynyard

(*Paulina draws back a curtain and
discovers Hermione as a statue.*)

For comfort I became a stone,
Silent where whispers stir,
I who had longed to be immune
To all tongues that infest the air.

I schooled the body where it dreamed,
I hushed all offices till I
Quiet and blind as Justice seemed
And I reigned in a still kingdom.

I banished motion, but have found
No simplicity in stone,
For one comes who believes and bends
Before me and makes me many things.

As one who stares and seems a prey
To the darkness of premonitions,
So in a fantasy he comes
And finds it already night.

He is a vagrant in my shadow,
An alien darkness, how should he know
I have conspired to this deathly
Dancing to unmoving music?

Both cause and image I became;
I am his innocence who grieves,
And while he tells all he believes
I of us both the mirror am.

I am the patience of a pool
Where all the planets sway, and I
Am the moon's self, a watery star
Beheld at night in a blue river.

I am the night where he is blind
And I the orbit of his prayers;
Quet above the suppliant hand,
I am the heaven of fixed stars.

I the elusive phoenix seem,
And a man is my age and fire,
For he has breathed me to this flame,
And I, seeming myself, seem fire.

Thus I who have not moved a limb,
Who feigned but changelessness and keep
Only the semblance that I was
Am all faces of time and sleep.

I had intended but to be
My picture in a stone, but I
Took shape of death and have become
Death, and all things come to me.

Death, in my varied majesty
I am astonished in flesh and stone
That you should be simplicity
Whose visage so resembles me.

SONG

How have I dreamed you, Lady,
Stricken among flames dark auburn:
O Lady, does your chimney burn?
Winds are moving dangerously;
I may be slow to warn;
Give me tidings in my concern:
O Lady, Lady, does your chimney burn?

If it would please you, Lady,
I could make your defences stubborn
Against odd wind and conflagration;
Or if flame owns you utterly
I might assure return
Better than ashes in your urn.
O Lady, Lady, does your chimney burn?

Or do you lack, Lady,
An intimate subaltern,
A tall sentry near your postern?
I shall fulfill as you employ me,
Turn as you bid me turn,
And be pleased if you so govern.
O Lady, Lady, does your chimney burn?

Or if I might be sea
To your green island laced with fern,
I should betide your coasts in turn
Learning your seasons, and so be
Fierce, as you pleased, or southern,

Wearing the air that you had worn.
O Lady, Lady, does your chimney burn?

Even, for your pleasure, Lady,
I could become your heat and learn
To rise for you when your mood is eastern,
And I should by such service, surely,
More than bare praises earn,
And all I received of you return;
O Lady, Lady, does your chimney burn?

SONG

Mirrors we lay wherein desire
Traded, by dark, conceits of fire;
As gardened minds whose delicacy
Could neither close with flesh nor flee,

Who watched by fire a bush inflect
What flame a window could reflect
Where dark and distance were control
So the leaves burned yet rested whole;

But flesh, dark forest to the mind,
Took at our breaths repeated wind
And from our eyes an equal glare:
Our distance broke and burned us there.

In married dark these fevers learn
Alternate loss; the bodies, worn
Indefinite, attend together
Night's pleasure and the press of weather.

The Dancing Bears

(1954)

FOR DIDO
—*marveling*

. . . la parole humaine est comme un chaudron félé où nous battons des mélodies à faire danser les ours, quand on voudrait attendrir les étoiles.

FLAUBERT

TOWER

Now I have come again
To the common country
Where all faces are mirrors and tell me
I return white-faced as the dawn.

Have I outrun belief
And walk in a superstition?
Ignorant and alone,
Without haste I went only

Among the innocent
Noon-laden fields, then
Among thickets, the way growing
Black and white and thorny,

And at the cockshut hour
—The summer dusk among
Its hedges drowsing—came
Upon the odor of apples,

Upon the darkling tower
Hung with no flutter of birds,
Puff of smoke or banner;
And when I called

No echo stirred nor answer,
Pin nor shutter, only
By the door a hanging wheel
In no wind was turning slowly.

Round and still as a finger
Laid upon lips, stone
Above stone, the tower. Its shadow
Fell as far as evening.

Dark spool wound within silence,
Ringed with stillness as with trees
—Birches stood hushed in the green air,
And moat-lapped apple trees.

Polished were the dark stones;
As ice they rose. Is it
That there the crevices
Run at neck-level always,

That where that water stands
Almost as ice, the rippling
Tails of salmon cut
The throats of all reflection?

I saw my body
As a smooth alien
On stones and water walking
Headless, not noticing;

And my head, drifting
Bereft of body, gave me
Again from every stone
My astonishment.

A pebble might have rung
A crash of seven years' portent,
On that water falling.
Or turn away the face.

But there was enough of portent
Folding that stony bobbin
If the failing light could limn
And limb such legerdemain.

And what if all motion
Were a web into that stance
And all shattering
But served that severance?

I cannot learn from mirrors
Or faces of this country
Which of me, head or body,
Still fronts itself there,

Still winds in unmoving dance
About itself while the shadows
Turn alike about flesh
About stone, about trees,

Till dizzy would the wind be
If wind there were; and yet
No apple falls, nor the green
Light like leaves from the trees;

And from somewhere unseen
The deceitful magpie sings,
"Love, love, oh lover,
Oh King live forever."

RUNES FOR A ROUND TABLE

Capricorn

Where darkness is
Once a mirror was
And I therein was king.
Bearded, lecherous,
Still I stand recalling
The windy cities
Like reeds wailing.

Aquarius

This is faithbearing:
All seas turning
On one's shoulders, to stand
Patiently as though painted
Though the fish be gone.

Pisces

Let the stars quaver
In night blue as a pool;
I rise, though the tide fall,
I turn, but I am still
And wiser than any water
In the eddying sky.

Aries

I bear suspicion
Like a golden fleece,
And horns like auguries
Curling into nothing;
On these the world has wheeled.

Taurus

White as a flower,
As a floating flower,
As a white child,
Eleven kings I wield;
Afloat in gentle water,
I trample on what is,
I am what is to be.

Gemini

He sinks when I rise,
He laughs when I die;
We twain are single
As the same rain falling
On two sides of a tree.

Cancer

Multitudes bow to me
On shores where no wave bows,
To me who slip sideways
In the heat of the day
With the blank stars for sand.

Leo

What greater ravage
Than this: to become
The multiple shield
Of the gilt marauder,
To hold a honeycomb,
Whose taste was for rage.

Virgo

Not so much as a song
In my most silver dream
Has ravished my ear.
Damage by beast and man
And by the scandalous sun
Sing out, but I am not there.

Libra

One man confronting two,
Each side on twelve legs walking,
Yet is no balance between:
The one outweighs the two,
For all hands are uneven
But the wheel is equal.

Scorpio

All unbidden
I offer an island;
Let the bidden man
Turn, flee like a season;
Mine is the turning end;
My bitterness, immortal,
Finds the mortal heel.

Sagittarius

All quarry flees. The arrow
Drawn always to my ear I still
Have not let fly, and yet they fall.

THE LADY WITH THE HERON

I walk athirst
In a month of rain;
Drought I learned
At the feet of a heron.

Green trees, full rivers;
Athirst I went,
With a shrieking bird
In the drawn breath.

At the only spring
When I went for water
I met a lady
And thirst I had none.

I say, at the fountain
There I met a lady,
She led a blue heron
By the beck of her hand.

Moon-wise the owl is,
The wren not tame,
But I unlearned patience
At the feet of a heron.

So deep a water
As those her eyes
Kissed I never
At the lip of April.

Drink, sir, she said,
Of so sweet water.
The bird was blind
That she led by a shadow.

Lady, I said,
Thirst is no longer.
But she led my eyes
By the beck of her hand.

Of her eyes I drank
And no other water.
Hope I unlearned
At the feet of a bird,

And saw no face
When I bent there;
Such saw I never
In other water.

My lips not wet,
Yet was she gone
Leading a heron
By the shade of her hand.

And my eyes thirst
On the birdless air;
Blindness I learned
At the feet of a heron.

WHEN I CAME FROM COLCHIS

When I came from Colchis
Where the spring fields lay green,
A land famed for fine linen,
Bounded northerly
By the glistering Caucasus,
By the Euxine westerly,

Most I spoke of fine linen
But did, in truth, tell something
Of Jason who had come sailing
And poised upon that shore
His fabulous excursion.
All turned the incredulous ear.

From Troy, over the water
Returning, I recounted
The tale of wrecked walls, but said
That gray waves lap and surround
That shore as any other.
With a shrewd smile they listened.

Now if, amazed, I come
From the deep bourn of your hand,
A stranger up from the sunned
Sea of your eyes, lady,
What fable should I tell them,
That they should believe me?

YOU, GENOESE MARINER

You, Genoese mariner,
Your face most perfectly
A mask about a vision,
Your eyes most clear when turned
On the bewildering west,
You, so your story goes,
Who believed that that direction
Toward which all breath and knowledge
Although their eyes cling elsewhere
Make ignorant declension,
Must by its own token,
Continuing, contain
A grammar of return,
A world's unknown dimension,
You, nevertheless, in search
Of gilt and spice, who fancied
Earth too circumscribed
To imagine and cradle,
Where no map had suspected,
The distances and marvels,
The unfingered world—
I whose face has become,
Oh mistaken sailor,
Suddenly a frame
For astonishment, stand
In the long light of wonder
Staring upon the shadows
That circle and return
From another's eyes,
I, after so long,
Who have been wrong as you.

FABLE

I am a mad precarious man
Making a prayer for folly
At the midnight and heartless hour,
Moon-beset, and my best of prayer
Is incontinently to complain
Upon a foolish story.

Long ago in a laurel wood—
Pray for the love of folly—
Once a lover, and he heartless,
And his lady, heartless likewise,
Loving, but without heart, there stood,
And they wept grievously.

He said: As though with a heart I grieve—
Pray for the poor in folly—
That we in whom great love there is
Should love less well than loveless bodies
For scarcely do we dare to love
Lest we love heartlessly.

She said: Some stint there must be done—
Pray for the lips of folly—
For how should we this pain abide
As thorough as though hearts we had
Yet suffer and love as though alone,
However entwined we be.

So they one heart between them made—
Pray for the hands of folly—

Of all heat and belief they knew,
For the sustenance whereof they two
Made tributary their own blood
And rejoiced heartily.

Dark it was in the laurel wood—
Pray for the eyes of folly—
A noise as of a breathing beast
Swung between them; when they kissed,
All about them it raged and played,
But nothing could they see.

Reverence overcame them then—
Pray for the heart of folly—
That they out of mere need could make
From nothing and a bit of dark
What had failed them from their creation,
And they sank upon knee.

And most religiously they swore—
Pray for the word of folly—
That never would they look upon
The warm marvel that beat between,
Lest, should their eyes prove so familiar,
It take offense and die.

So they took heart, and the heart, grown wild—
Pray for the limbs of folly—
Would lunge on the hollow dark like pain,
And then, till love came round again,
Lie and be gentled like a child
And feed on intimacy.

Almost nine hours they lived at ease—
Pray for the life of folly—
Yet dawn, ubiquitous, could watch
How they grew curious till each,

Unknown to the other, raised his eyes
Out of their dark and pity

And saw within the other's eyes—
Pray for the bells of folly—
Where they all tenderness had set,
Burning upon the day, a great
Bull-shouldered beast with horns of brass
Who cried in fury,

Who lunged between them like all pain—
Pray for the death of folly—
In mortal rage, till brass and beast
Gored nothing but the ground at last,
And empty, where a heart had been,
Love's body lay.

Ghosts are heartless that tease the blood—
Pray for the soul of folly—
And ghostly as a coil of rain
Heartless they stood once again,
Day-stricken in the laurel wood,
And they wept grievously.

I am a sullen unseemly man—
Pray now no more for folly—
Who in the bleak and tolling hour
Walk like a chime without a tower,
Rending a story, and complain
Heartless and foolishly.

THE PASSION

In that garden at evening
We could not speak save in prayer
Unto each other saying,
"Each other's will be done";
Nor could we walk under
Bare thorn but the branches
Unnaturally would compose
Over our heads a crown.
    Non enim sciunt quid faciunt

Truly, strong bulls of Bashan
Had beset us round;
Our doom, though falsely, had been
Foretold, and where we came
Hands were washed of our end;
And there was that fretful spouse
Had suffered because of us,
Many things in a dream.
    Non enim sciunt quid faciunt

Each of us, we knew,
Must be unto the other
The singular cross; yet how
Could either of us hang painful
Upon the other, either
Upon the other weigh
As burden? Merrily
We went out to that hill.
Non enim sciunt quid faciunt

We heard the nails scream
In the wood as they were drawn
Out from the last time,
And felt their pain; the cry
You swore was old affection .
And smiled upon the sound
Not woodenly, but I turned
My wooden face away.
  Non enim sciunt quid faciunt

Three hours we hung as though
To veil the sun; thereafter
The earth shook; and, although
You said it was not real,
The dark was ours: no other
Voices, at last no thirst;
Doubt not, love, though the first
Death is original.
  Non enim sciunt quid faciunt

On the stroke of our absence,
They say, the sainted dead
Rose from their double patience
In jealousy, for we seemed
Our own heaven. Through the rifted
Temple veil we saw only
Darkness, and virgins darkly
Coming with lamps untrimmed.
  Non enim sciunt quid faciunt

They led us away
To this place we were to harrow
And rise from, the third day,
And howso scripture be truthful,
Yet this pain we pass through,
Though shared, consumes us by
Dividing infinitely,
Is at all times eternal.
        Non enim sciunt quid faciunt

MARGERY'S SONG

I am a jill-whisper
And a cold sister
And a windy daughter
With hawthorn in my hair.

Five fingers of thin willow
Flicker my preferment;
I go feat but draughty
With a ghost of rag about me.

A nimble bird I saw:
Ruses were its children;
And friendly was the wind
But spoke me hungerly.

A little coin, a morsel,
Give me for my sleeking
For fear trespass should busy
Hands no better than bony.

Whose dish is cold and clever?
I saw a bone shiver.
In name of shadows bleating
Yet meatily the mouth feeds.

Soul is thin confusion.
I am vagary
Snared in a bony body
With hawthorn in my hair.

SONG OF THE MAD MENAGERIE

I on whom the wild sun
Upon unvaried journey
Burned with jealousy
Because of my unreason,

Know I was legendary.
On straw I lie down.
Wise hand, be wary:
My rage is uneven.

In a cautious country
The wild shadows came down
As though athirst, came softly
And drank of the clear moon.

But the wind was tamed away,
But all the palms fell down.
The bright aviary
Sings, "O daughters of Zion."

Thirst is yet necessary:
The lean shade comes down
Of my own savagery
To sip my dry distraction.

Hands, befriend cautiously:
Now I pace alone
That mad menagerie,
The body behind bone.

SONG OF MARVELS

The day is down.
All a shiver of gold,
Age talks in the trees.
All faces rise out of the sea.

Think, think of the marvel:
One time there was a beggar
Loved a great lady
For the sake of white hands.

I hear a whisper break
Cavernous upon coral;
The hours like fishes
Wheel in amber undersea.

Sing, sing of the marvel:
A beggar with his two hands
Killed a great lady
For the love of patience.

I see the speech of leaves
That lisp in the late garden
And eyes like fishes
In deep amber waving.

Sing, sing of the marvel:
Our hands are fathomless,
Our eyes shake in the gold,
All for the love of patience.

SONG OF THREE SMILES

Let me call a ghost,
Love, so it be little:
In December we took
No thought for the weather.

Whom now shall I thank
For this wealth of water?
Your heart loves harbors
Where I am a stranger.

Where was it we lay
Needing no other
Twelve days and twelve nights
In each other's eyes?

Or was it at Babel
And the days too small
We spoke our own tongue
Needing no other?

If a seed grow green
Set a stone upon it
That it learn thereby
Holy charity.

If you must smile
Always on that other,
Cut me from ear to ear
And we all smile together.

SONG OF THE NEW FOOL

Let the sea and all her women
With their combs and white horses,
Their mirrors and shells, the green-flaming
Bushes, the bull-necked hills,

The uncombed crags, and the trees
Shading their leopards and thrushes,
The shadows and loud peacocks,
Rocks, and the laughing geese,

And the fires, and the fire that stood
Still over Jericho,
The stars and the wet moon,
And the day and the night

(But caution: for the west wind
Is secret, the west wind's hunger
All love and ghost
May not satisfy)

And laughter and the unicorn
Come in the morning
While the air is a blue girl
And eat from my hand.

For I filled my hands
With fists and cursed till the bone
Heart of the world broke;
And my hands are tender.

EAST OF THE SUN AND
WEST OF THE MOON

Say the year is the year of the phoenix.
Ordinary sun and common moon,
Turn as they may, are too mysterious
Unless such as are neither sun nor moon
Assume their masks and orbits and evolve
Neither a solar nor a lunar story
But a tale that might be human. What is a man
That a man may recognize, unless the inhuman
Sun and moon, wearing the masks of a man,
Weave before him such a tale as he
—Finding his own face in the strange story—
Mistakes by metaphor and calls his own,
Smiling, as on a familiar mystery?

The moon was thin as a poor man's daughter
At the end of autumn. A white bear came walking
On a Thursday evening at the end of autumn,
Knocked at a poor man's door in a deep wood,
And, "Charity," when the man came he said,
"And the thin hand of a girl have brought me here.
Winter will come, and the vixen wind," he said,
"And what have you but too many mouths to feed,
Oh what have you but a coat like zither-strings
To ward that fury from your family?
But I though wintry shall be bountiful
Of furs and banquets, coins like summer days,
Grant me but the hand of your youngest daughter."

"By a swooning candle, in my porchless door,
While all I wedded or sired huddle behind me,
The night unceremonious with my hair,
I know I cut a poor figure," the man said;
"And I admit that your cajolery
(For opulence was once my setting-on)
Finds me not deaf; but I must ask my daughter.
And no, she says. But come again on Thursday:
She is more beautiful than the story goes,
And a girl who wants a week for her persuading
Merits that slow extravagance," he said.
Further in autumn by a week's persuading
The youngest girl on a white bear went riding.

The moon played in a painted elder tree;
He said, when they had gone a while, "We walk
In a night so white and black, how can you tell
My shoulder from a moon-struck hill, my shadow
From the towering darkness; are you not afraid?"
And, "You are thin and colorful who ride
Alone on a white and monstrous thing; suppose
I rose up savage in a desolate place;
Are you not afraid?" And, "What if I were to wander
Down a black ladder, in a trope of death,
Through seven doors all of black ice, and come
On a land of hyperbole, stiff with extremes;
Would it not make the hair rise on your head?"

The wind with moonlit teeth rippled and sulked
In the paper trees, but three times "No," she said.
"Oh then hold fast by the hair of my shoulders,"
He said; "hold fast my hair, my savage hair;
And let your shadow as we go hold fast
The hair of my shadow, and all will be well."
Later than owls, all night, a winter night,
They traveled then, until the screaming wind
Fell behind or dead, till no stars glittered

86

In the headlong dark; and each step dark and long
As falling in the valley of the blind;
Yet all the while she felt her yellow hair
Hang loose at her shoulders, as though she stood still.

They came before daylight to a stone hill
Steep as a pier glass, where no shrub grew,
Nor grass rustled, nor breeze stirred before dawn.
When the bear knocked, a door swung wide. Their eyes
Enormous with the dark, a hall they entered
That blazed between mirrors, between pilasters
Of yellow chrysolite; on walls of brass
Gold branches of dead genealogies
Clutched candles and wild torches whence the flames
Rose still as brilliants. Under a fiery
Garnet tree with leaves of glass, sunken
In a pool of sea-green beryl as in still water
A gold salmon hung. And no sound came.

The wall healed behind them. When she turned,
The wall steep as a pier glass, the door
Vanished like a face in ruffled water,
And they stood dumb in the echoing light
While no flame crackled, no water fell. They passed
Between the rows of burning, between the rings
Of extinct animals that stared from sockets
In the braziered walls; hour upon hour,
Hall upon blazing hall, and came at last
Through obsequious curtains to a closed room
Where she descended; at a beck of his head
A gold table leapt from the air; she dined
That night on lapwing and wine of pomegranates.

The bear had gone. She touched a silver bell.
She stood straightway in a white chamber
By a bed of lapis lazuli. Red agate
And yellow chrysolite the floors. A white

Carnelian window gave upon cut hills
Of amethyst and yellow serpentine
Pretending summer; when she stood naked there
Her nakedness from the lighted stones
Sprang a thousand times as girl or woman,
Child or staring hag. The lamps went black;
When she lay down to sleep, a young man came
Who stayed all night in the dark beside her
But was gone before dawn came to that country.

Nightly he came again. Once he said,
"I am the white bear, who once was a man;
In a christian body, in a green kingdom
One time I had dominion. Now I keep
Not so much as the shadow that I had,
And my own shape only by dark; by day
Compelled I am to that pale beast. Let it be
Ensample to your forbearance: here love
Must wander blind or with mistaken eyes,
For dissolution walks among the light
And vision is the sire of vanishing."
What love soever in the dark there were,
Always at daylight she wakened alone.

By day she walked in the espaliered garden
Among pheasants and clear flowers; she said,
"What if these pheasants amble in white glass,
Ducks strut ridiculous in stone, the streams
Slither nowhere in beryl; why should I
Complain of such inflexible content,
Presume to shudder at such serenity,
Who walk in some ancestral fantasy,
Lunar extravagance, or lost pagoda
That dreams of no discipline but indolence?
What shall be rigid but gems and details
While all dimensions dance in the same air?
And what am I if the story be not real?

But what it is," she said, "to wander in silence,
Though silence be a garden. What shall I say,
How chiseled the tongue soever, and how schooled
In sharp diphthongs and suasive rhetorics,
To the echoless air of this sufficiency?
Where should I find the sovereign aspirate
To rouse in this world a tinkle of syllables,
Or what shall I sing to crystal ears, and where
All songs drop in the air like stones; oh what
Shall I do while the white tongued flowers shout
Impossible silence on the impossible air
But wander with my hands over my ears?
And what am I if the story be not real?

He says the place is innocent; and yet
I may not see his face; claims he is held
Equivocating between prince and beast
By the ministrations of an evil stepdame,
But such might be mere glittering deviltry.
Here is no nightly moon or tidal water
But mornings miming at mutability
Where all stands new at noon and nothing fades
Down the perfect amber of the afternoons;
All, simultaneous and unwearied, comes
Guesting again at evening. But a day
Must dwindle before dawn be real again;
And what am I if the story be not real?"

She said at night when he lay beside her,
"Why should I raise the singular dissent
Who delight in an undiminished country
Where all that was or shall be transitory
Stands whole again already? Yet I sigh
For snipes to whir and fall, for hawks to fall,
For one more mortal crimson that will fade,
For one glimpse of the twisted holly tree
Before my mother's door, and the short-lived

Wren by my mother's window, and the tame crane
Walking in shallow water. I would learn
Whether I dreamed then or walk now in a dream,
For what am I if the story be not real?"

Suddenly where no sound had been she heard
A distant lisp and crumble, like a wave,
Like the whisper of tidal water, emulous
Of its own whispers: his echoing heart. "Shall I
Pace an eternity of corridors,
Alone among sad topaz, the reflections
Flickering only on your emptiness,
And the soundlessness be like a sound of mourning,
That seemed a sound of joy? Nevertheless,
Go you shall if you wish; but promise,
Lest a malicious word undo us both,
Never to walk or talk alone," he said,
"With your mother, who is as wise as you."

It was a Sunday. Gold on the glass leaves.
She sat in the garden on the white bear's shoulders.
She touched a silver bell, and instantly
Saw the swaying of incorrigible meadows
Ripening, a green wind playful in barley,
The holly, contorted at her mother's door,
The fluttering wren—the brief feathers
Provisional about mortality—
At her mother's window, the tame crane walking
As though not real where the real shallows ran.
She had descended; the bear was gone;
She heard the whistling grass, and the holly leaves
Saying, "Your mother, who is wise as you."

She was greeted like a lost season.
Daylong she walked again in affluent summer,
But one day walked at last aside, and talked
Alone with her mother, who was wise as she.

"Equivocation between prince and beast,
The ministrations of an evil stepdame,
Might be a devilish tale; how could you tell,"
Her mother said, "should it be the devil's self
Or some marvel of ugliness you lay beside?
Take, better than advice, this end of candle
To light when he sleeps next you in the dark;
Only be careful that no drops fall."
The grass might whistle under the holly leaves.

On a day of no clouds he came to fetch her.
It was a Sunday. A soft wind stroking
The fields already white almost to harvest.
"Shall we not ride a while in the mortal air
Before we go," he asked, "for the love of fading?
But wish, when you are weary, for the sound
Of the silver bell, and we shall instantly
Be home again. Did all happen as I said?"
"Yes," she said, "how might it be otherwise?"
"Did you, then, walk aside with your mother?" he asked;
"Did you listen to your mother's advice?"
"Oh no," she said. "Then all may yet be well."
But she wished for the sound of the silver bell.

That night when she was sure he slept
She rose in the dark and struck light
To the end of candle, and held it above his face.
What blaze was this, what prince shaming with beauty
The sun peerless at noon? The dazzled stones
Seemed each a blond particular summer wringing
In the one thirst the lion and the nightingale.
The shadows bowed; they fell down amazed.
"And I with my foolish arm upraised . . .
But love so beggars me of continence,
Either I must kiss him or die," she said,
And bent, therewith, and kissed his head. Three times
The tallow folly from the candle fell.

"Oh why must all hope resolve to vanity?"
Waking, he cried; "Why could you not entertain
A curious patience but for one whole year,
For then had we been saved, and my spell broken.
Now this kingdom must shatter and I depart
For the wheeling castle of my stepmother
And marry a princess with a nose three ells long,
When I might have married you." "Oh love," she cried,
"May I not learn the way and follow you?"
"There is no way there that a body might follow;
Farther than dreams that palace lies,
East of the sun and west of the moon, girt
With rage of stars for sea. There no one comes."

She seemed to sleep, for she woke again
On a usual morning in a different world,
Bright grass blowing, birds loud in the trees;
That precious kingdom, that charmed lover
Gone. She was kneeling under a willow
In her salt tears. When she had called
And cried till she was weary she walked on
Slowly, walked the length of a day, and seemed
None the more weary for all her walking
But traveled, it seemed, in a landscape of exceptions
Where no evening came but a shadowy
Skeptical bird who settled in a tree
And sang, "All magic is but metaphor."

Under a crag, when it should have been evening,
Where there should have been shadows, by an apple tree,
She saw a hag who laughed to herself and tossed
A golden apple. "Good day, hag," she said.
"Can you tell me how I might find the castle
That lies east of the sun and west of the moon?"
"Whoever comes and calls me hag, haggard
May she sit also, unless it be the lady
Who should marry the prince there. Are you she?

Yes, she says. Yet the way I cannot tell.
Take, rather, this gold apple, mount this horse
To ride to ask my sister, and once there,
Tap him behind the left ear; he will come home."

Long she rode as the patience of stones
And saw again, when it should have been evening,
A hag who played with a golden carding comb.
"If withering were a signature of wisdom,
I were a miracle of sagacity,"
She said, "my brow invisible with laurel,
But I am bare parchment where a word might be,
And any road that might lead to that castle
Is a thing I never knew. All I can offer
By way of blessing is this gold carding comb,
But you might ask my sister; take my own horse.
When he has brought you where she sits, tap him
Behind the left ear; he will come home again."

The third hag said, "I have been young as you,
And shall be so again, unless the stars
Tell lies in the shifty dark, but whether
More pleasure is to be young and pass for fair
Or to be haggard and seem knowledgeable,
I am too wise to choose, and yet the way
That castle lies is a thing I never knew;
But there you will come, late or never. I give you,
Beside that wisdom, this golden spinning wheel,
And if you wish, you may ride my own horse
To ask the East Wind. When you are there,
Tap the beast once behind the left ear,
And he will be off and come to me again."

Oh then she rode such waste of calendars
She should have found the end of weariness
But came instead to the house of the East Wind.
"Oh Wind," she called, "which way would you blow,

Which way might I follow to come to the castle
That lies east of the sun and west of the moon?"
"I, bold of wing beyond the glimpse of morning,
Have found the dark where no birds sleep,
Have shivered and returned, have many times
Heard of that castle, but never blown so far
Nor learned the way. But I have a brother," he said,
"An infinite voyager: be pleased to sit
Between my shoulders and I shall take you there."

Though faster then than summoned ghosts they flew,
Long was that journey as the wisdom of owls
Before they came to the roof of the West Wind.
"For all I am prodigious of voyages,
Whistle heyday and holiday, make light
Of the poor limbs of summer and have sailed
Beyond the hueless sighing of drowned days
Into the dark where no shades sigh,
Have shuddered and come home a different way,
Unholy be the whisper of my name
If ever I were a wind about that tower
Or knew the way; but come with me," he said:
"I have a brother who has blown further than I."

"I might shriek till the world was small
As a turtle's egg; I have whipped my savagery
A pride of days beyond where the world ends
In burning, into the dark where no flames twitch,
Have blessed myself and hastily blown elsewhere,
But never glimpsed wrack nor wisp of that castle,
And whether there be any such place at all
I gravely doubt; but I have a brother
Wields the gale that flaps the chittering dead
Beyond where the world ends in ice; be sure
Unless his storm can shiver your conundrum
It is a thing unknown." The South Wind's wings
Howled, till they came to the door of the North Wind.

"Oh once," he roared, "I blew an aspen leaf
Beyond the glimmering world, over
The glass eaves of time, into that dark
Where no ice gleams; there, bristling, found that other
Wind of fear, but a rage stayed me until
The star-lashed sea, until I found the castle
That lies east of the sun and west of the moon.
But never I told a soul, for there I lay
Three weeks, frail as the aspen leaf, on the wild
Shore before I dared blow home again.
But if you be the lady that you claim,
Stay while I rest tonight and I shall try
Tomorrow if I can fly so far again."

Who has outflown the nightmare? Yet fast
Almost as she they flew in the morning
Beyond all boreal flickerings, headlong
Over the glass caves of time and found
The breathless dark where no souls stir,
But hair in another wind; broke, almost blind,
At last over a mad famished sea;
Then long as unspoken love they whirled.
But he wearied. The waves snapped at his knees,
The dog-toothed waves, till he whispered, "My wings fail,"
Sinking. But she cried, "I see a white shore,
A shadowy pinnacle that may be the castle
That lies east of the sun and west of the moon."

What if the breakers gulped and craved his thighs?
Where he had set her on the white shore
He fell forward and slept. Already
A foot beyond the frustrate sea there drowsed
Silence of forests, indolent, rimmed
With flutter of birches like birds in the tender
Sun, with thirsty osiers, pale hawthorn,
Perpetual apple trees, the capricious-limbed.
She saw in that light how the castle vanished

95

Above fancy among faithful clouds,
Saw the door, but nowhere near the door she went,
But sat under a guelder-rose and sang
"Ah, well-a-day," and played with the gold apple.

Till from an upper window of the castle
A princess with a nose three ells long
Called, "Who are you, singing 'well-a-day'
Under my window; and oh what will you take
And give me that golden apple?" "I am a lady
Of foreign ways singing to my own hair
A dirge for diminishing, under a pale tree,
Am a hazard waif blown from the scapegrace sea,
Am an aspen leaf; but nothing you own
Will I exchange for this gold apple,
Unless it should be that I might sleep tonight
Alone all night in his room with the prince
Who lives in this castle." And that could be arranged.

But she was returned, for earnest of gold,
Only a sleeping body and a sleep:
When she was led at evening into his room
Already he lay sleeping; for all she cried
His name aloud, for all she cried and kissed
His face and forehead, all night he lay sleeping.
What might she be but chorus to a dream,
But one who strokes a dream of chrysolite,
Glass pheasants, ducks ridiculous in stone,
A gold salmon in a beryl pool,
As reliquary, as meager communicance
Till daylight, then departs and sits again
By the tower and plays with the gold carding comb?

"Nothing whatever will I take," she said
When the princess called, "for my gold carding comb,
But to sleep tonight by the same prince."
But where was the unrecking fantasy,

The concord of distraught belief
She had named for love and understood by love,
If when she lay, and the second time, beside him
Nothing would answer to her kiss but sleep?
Must she before she wake still find a dream
Wherein she lay beside him, and he, waking,
Dreamed still of her? Although beside him, dream
Of yet more fortunate wakenings; till daylight;
Then sing by a gold spinning wheel, dreaming?

"I am a thirsty lady wishing I walked
Beside no water but a pool of beryl;
I sing to drown the silence of far flowers
And though I am deaf to all sounds other
Than a deafening heart in a distant room, I dream
I wander with my hands over my ears."
She argued with the princess as yesterday,
Parted with the gold spinning wheel. Oh must
Love's many mansions, the patient honeycomb
Of hope unlearn their heavens and at a sleep
Triply be consigned to cerements,
Or must salvation shrink to the unlikely
Monstrance of another's wakening?

Suppose the requisite vigil. Say one lay
Two nights awake beside the prince's room,
Heard crying there, as toward a vanishing spectre,
Told the prince, and he, thus wise against potions
The third night, sleepless, with wide arms received her,
Calling, "Oh love, is blessedness a risk
So delicate in time, that it should be
Tonight you find me? Tomorrow, always tomorrow
It is that my stepmother was to prevail,
It is that I was to marry that other princess.
But we are the sense of dawn beneath pretence
Of an order of darkness. Now lie in wisdom, mindful
Only of love, and leave to me tomorrow."

In the morning, to proud stepdame and coy princess,
"Call me a wry intransigent, a glass
Of fickle weathers, but what care I," he said,
"For decorum, though it be my wedding day?
Shall I be yoked to an unproven woman?
But who she may be can wash this shirt of mine,
Stained with three drops of tallow, white again
As once it was, she and no other lady
Will I marry. All wet the hands who wish;
All beat the board; all wring the linen; all wash
In the one water." Howsoever the princess
Dipped and wrung, the stains ran gray; or stepdame
Scrubbed, the shirt grew black as knavery.

"There is a girl outside the castle door,"
One said who loitered there and watched; "perhaps
She if she tried might wash it white again."
But vexed stepdame and angry princess
Raged then and screamed, "No no! Shall we have a tattered
Waif with outlandish ways for rival, and we
With our royal hands in water?" Yet the prince
Answered, "Let her come in, whoever she be."
She dipped the linen and once drew it forth
White as a leper; drew it forth again
White as blown snow; a third time raised it
Spotless, white as the violent moon; she said,
"How should I not, since all pallor is mine?"

The moon was musing in her high chamber
Among nine thousand mirrors. "Oh what am I,"
She cried, "but a trick of light, and tropically?
I walk in a wild charactry of night,
In a game of darkness figurative with tapers,
Toying with apples, and come upon myself
More often than is meet for sanity.
Oh, who would be shown, save in analogy,
  —What for gold handsels and marvelous equerry—

As three hags sitting under an apple tree?
But I walk multifarious among
My baubles and horses; unless I go in a mask
How shall I know myself among my faces?"

"All metaphor," she said, "is magic. Let
Me be diverted in a turning lantern,
Let me in that variety be real.
But let the story be an improvisation
Continually, and through all repetition
Differ a little from itself, as though
Mistaken; and I a lady with foreign ways
To sing therein to my own hair." To the sun,
"You who tomorrow are my Pentecost,
Come dance with me—oh but be white, be wintry;
Oh lest I fall an utter prey to mirrors,
Be a white bear," she said "and come a-walking,
And ask my hand. I am a peasant's daughter."

Is it for nothing that a troupe of days
Makes repeated and perpetual rummage
In the lavish vestry; or should sun and moon,
Find mortality too mysterious,
Naked and with no guise but its own,
—Unless one of immortal gesture come
And by a mask should show it probable—
Believe a man, but not believe his story?
Say the year is the year of the phoenix.
Now, even now, over the rock hill
The tropical, the lucid moon, turning
Her mortal guises in the eye of a man,
Creates the image in which the world is.

ON THE SUBJECT OF POETRY

I do not understand the world, father.
By the millpond at the end of the garden
There is a man who slouches listening
To the wheel revolving in the stream, only
There is no wheel there to revolve.

He sits in the end of March, but he sits also
In the end of the garden; his hands are in
His pockets. It is not expectation
On which he is intent, nor yesterday
To which he listens. It is a wheel turning.

When I speak, father, it is the world
That I must mention. He does not move
His feet nor so much as raise his head
For fear he should disturb the sound he hears
Like a pain without a cry, where he listens

I do not think I am fond, father,
Of the way in which always before he listens
He prepares himself by listening. It is
Unequal, father, like the reason
For which the wheel turns, though there is no wheel.

I speak of him, father, because he is
There with his hands in his pockets, in the end
Of the garden listening to the turning
Wheel that is not there, but it is the world,
Father, that I do not understand.

PROTEUS

By the splashed cave I found him. Not
(As I had expected) patently delusive
In a shape sea-monstrous, terrible though sleeping,
To scare all comers, nor as that bronze-thewed
Old king of Pharos with staring locks,
But under a gray rock, resting his eyes
From futurity, from the blinding crystal
Of that morning sea, his face flicked with a wisp
Of senile beard, a frail somnolent old man.

Who would harness the sea-beast
To the extravagant burden of his question
Must find him thus dreaming of his daughters,
Of porpoises and horses; then pitiless
Of an old man's complaints, unawed
At what fierce beasts are roused under his grasp,
Between the brutal ignorance of his hands
Must seize and hold him till the beast stands again
Manlike but docile, the neck bowed to answer.

I had heard in seven wise cities
Of the last shape of his wisdom: when he,
Giver of winds, father as some said
Of the triple nightmare, from the mouth of a man
Would loose the much-whistled wind of prophecy.
The nothing into which a man leans forward
Is mother of all restiveness, drawing
The body prone to falling into no
Repose at last but the repose of falling.

Wherefore I had brought foot to his island
In the dead of dawn, had picked my way
Among the creaking cypresses, the anonymous
Granite sepulchres; wherefore, beyond these,
I seized him now by sleeping throat and heel.
What were my life, unless I might be stone
To grasp him like the grave, though wisdom change
From supposition to savage supposition;
Unless the rigor of mortal hands seemed deathly?

I was a sepulchre to his pleadings,
Stone to his arguments, to his threats;
When he leapt in a bull's rage
By horn and tail I held him; I became
A mad bull's shadow, and would not leave him;
As a battling ram he rose in my hands;
My arms were locked horns that would not leave his horns;
I was the cleft stick and the claws of birds
When he was a serpent between my fingers.

Wild as heaven erupting into a child
He burst under my fists into a lion;
By mane and foot I grappled him;
Closer to him than his own strength I strained
And held him longer. The sun had fought
Almost to noon when I felt the beast's sinews
Fail, the beast's bristles fall smooth
Again to the skin of a man. I loosed him then.
The head he turned toward me wore a face of mine.

Here was no wisdom but my own silence
Echoed as from a mirror; no marine
Oracular stare but my own eyes
Blinded and drowned in their reflections;
No voice came but a voice we shared, saying,
"You prevail always, but, deathly, I am with you

Always." I am he, by grace of no wisdom,
Who to no end battles the foolish shapes
Of his own death by the insatiate sea.

COLLOQUY AT PENIEL

Countenance like lightning, why do you stand
In ebony raiment after no invocation
Suddenly where I knew no face, as though
You had stood so forever?

                 —Say that the light
That is today, after so long becomes me,
Or that love's pleading incense that rose once
For mercy pleads now no longer, whereupon
The air conceives new clarity, and there
Suddenly I am visible. But know
I was the urgency that framed that love
And made it cry for mercy, the question
And the voice of the woman whispering, "Be content,
Be content."
          I am that which you lost
Behind you which you seek before you, for I
Am certain: sullen under your gaiety
And still its root and entrepreneur; footloose,
Not musical, but moving in all your music,
Assumed in all apostrophes.
                  Think of me
As of a dusk through which no herds go home,
Quiet, perhaps, yet inexcusably
Disquieting, with a voice of infinite patience,
Gentle until resisted, like sheep bells
In the next valley.
             And I am he
With whom on a desperate hill, because I was
The closest combatant, always last night

You wrestled, as with the angel of your dark,
And overcame, yet in defeat who found
Such re-creation, always I rose with dawn
Enlarged by falling, as though I were the angel,
Equally, of your day. Yet one day
—Heaven and hills having endured—your arm,
Hopeless long since of conquest, will strike upon
Fatal surprise and end me there; and through
The evening slanting always at hand among
Unstartled trees, under a world of birds
Settling like dust despite the clang of triumph,
It will be your body that will fall.

DECEMBER: OF APHRODITE

Whatever the books may say, or the plausible
Chroniclers intimate: that I was mad,
That an unsettling wind that season
Fretted my sign and fetched up violence
From the vagaries of dream, or even that pride
Is a broad road with few turnings, do not
Believe them. In her name I acted.

(Vidal once, the extravagant of heart,
For the love of a woman went mad, mad as a dog,
And the wolves ate him; Hercules, crazed
By that jealous goddess, murdered his children;
Samson, from a woman's lap, woke blinded,
Turning a mill in Gaza; Adam, our father,
Eating from his wife's hand, fell from the garden.)

Not that from heaven she twisted my tenderness
Into a hand of rage, nor because she delighted
In burnt offering, I in my five senses
Cut throats of friends, burned the white harvest, waged
Seven months' havoc even among
Her temples; but because she waited always
There in the elegant shell, asking for sweetness.

And though it was in her name the land was ravaged,
Spilled and dishonored, let it not be said
That by her wiles it was done, nor that she gave
That carnage her blessing. All arrogant demons
Pretending changelessness, who came first when she called,

Have faded and are spent, till out of the strong,
Without death, she conjured the honeycomb.

She sits at evening under a gray arch
Where many marvels fell, where all has fallen:
The blue over her dolphins, the poplar leaves,
The cold rain, all but the grave myrtle
And the rings of her ringdoves. The doge of one calendar
Would give her a name of winter, but where I stand
In the hazed gold of her eyes, the world is green.

CANSO

Was there truly in that afternoon
No sorcery, when the leaves between us
In the October garden fell like words
Through the long sun before the gathering winter;
Was there no enchantment but your imputation?
I was a name inconstant; I had come,
Unlooked for, from the shifting sea, my face
A field for doubting, my tales untrustworthy;
You believed, and therewith I was credible.

And that stern evening, speaking of snares
Where the hunter had fallen, where even the wise might fall,
Or speaking, in November, of primroses,
When doubt possessed me, and my eyes fell
To stones, half trusting in stones, and my mind fell
To a merciless winter of bleak words, yet you
Beyond words believed me to be a gentle
Season, and I, as from sleep returning,
Was thence the sign and green wind of spring.

You are the tender hazel and diviner
Whose faith is delicacy; yet had you
Believed me anything but what I was
I should have come—still without violence
But gently as that legendary beast
The unicorn, who did not exist
· Until conceived in the mind of a virgin—
Through the woods of change, and laid down my head
To fill the lap and hand of your supposition.

For you, by all the faiths in which we figure,
Are undeceivable: we are not ourselves
And I but a shadow in your superstition
Unless love be an imagination
Framing the singular metaphor of coherence
In the dying riot of random generation,
Unless it be the passion of an order
Informs you so to this innocent
Authority, this peculiar knowledge.

And have you not become, by much believing,
Yourself the prime breath, the infusion of the real
Upon this dust? I walked incredible
As death, a gaunt preposterous ghost, until
Your creed included me among the living:
But not until I had, as from despair,
Abandoned claim to all the probable senses
And had become your trope and tenet merely,
Could I inherit the familiar body.

I am renewed as you imagine me
For all the orders which love believes
Are the one order. There, listening, the child
In love with wonder, ascribing contradictions
To the different gesture of an heroic world,
Attributing the bruited failure
To an alien but more excellent mode
Of triumph, creates a possible
World for the impossible legionary.

There forlorn clown and painted masquer
Do not move in a demonstration merely,
Cynical, of the necessity of error,
But perform an ordered rage of jubilation,
And the eye in love with compassion believes
The figures of compassion: the mad girl
Mourning her father, the fretted prince delaying

Particular confusion till the confusion
Of death be absolute and general.

The idiom of order is celebration,
An elegance to redeem the graceless years;
So those the nine-years-enraged for a filched doxy
Who contend forever in the fanciful song
Are the real, and those who with tangible
Bronze fought are now the unbelievable dead,
Their speech inconceivable, their voyages in vain,
Their deeds inaccurate, save as they coincide
With the final tale, the saving celebration.

But you, believing, name a new paradigm
That existed, nonetheless, before
The hour of your believing: for the order
Is, although the place where it exist
Be nowhere but a possibility;
And your believing spins continually
Its own newness: as time continues
Out of the possibility of itself.
Time is a creature like the unicorn.

It is by your faith that I believe, I am,
Therein is genesis, as though a man,
In love with existence, should bring to belief
A divinity, an imagination
That might move upon the idea of nothing
And image a man; as though a man could make
A mirror out of his own divinity,
Wherein he might believe himself, and be.
So, in your articles, we love, you are.

And our hands are a shape of confidence,
A gesture of releasing, where joy is always
Young as its own beginning. Thus the falling
Water is confident and falls, thus summer

Confidently fails, and both are new
As often as they fall. Believing is
Conception, is without artifice the making
Perpetually new, is that first holy
Aura and ordinance of creation.

I have pronounced you the single luminary,
And we are housed in an embrace of whiteness,
But shadows would threaten and the dark descend
In all the rooms where we believe. Oh love,
Believe this candor indivisible,
That I, perfected in your love, may be,
Against all dissolution sovereign,
Endlessly your litany and mirror,
About your neck the amulet and song.

CANSO

Must there be in the continuum and whorl
Of love always this whisper, on the tender
Horizon this supposition always,
A boreal shudder of feared light, a voice
That in my own voice cries to you, "Love, love,
Must you, in time more compromised than I,
In time be spoken from me, and I be left
To sit alone as it were forever,
Telling over the scandal that is time
In this dark room where the pictures hang
On the silence as though it were a wall?"

Or why should it be that we walk always
Slowly as though to lag long after time
And be alone there, that we perform
All of affection with a ceremony
Of more than patience, as though there were to be
Presently an end, or that I see you
Always, my eyes clear as on that day
When in fear of winter we watched the high ridge,
The tilted plain complacent in such summer,
Knowing we saw them for the last time, and love
Became itself a sense of leave-taking?

If you, if you my word and so my life
And so the mode and vessel of my death,
Should die before me, I would not go
—Although turned phantom by your truancy—
Calling the earth of you; neither, impelled
By what pain soever, with a zeal

As of an antiquarian, cull, compose
At last a vacancy of you and there become
An impresario of emptiness
Swaying before defection. What are the patterned
Potsherds to him who knows what wine there was?

It is not the comforts of a chiliast,
Nor of a mind mnemonic and apart
As an old man rocking in his doorway at
Irrelevant evening that I would wish to hear
Mumbling, "There was a world, there was, as it were,
A world wherein she walked once and was loved.
Is this, among worlds, not similar? And if
A tree wherein a throstle sang should lose
Not leaves but the bird only, would it not
Be, though without that singing, yet as green
As ever?" It would be the tree had died.

And what profit would there be to me then
In the lure of song, the twanged incantation,
Which on a time so played on savagery
With order, that the beasts came: phoenix and sow,
Cat, unicorn, chimaera came, swimming
Through the incredibility of themselves
As through the air, to sit in a round,
To hear, to hear a wish? Unless they might
By virtue of the same order, as by love,
But changelessly, stand listening so forever
And there be real in the ultimate song.

Unless you also in that animal
Constraint of death having become
Incredible, might nevertheless by such
Enchantment, as once by love, but changelessly,
Be tamed out of that emptiness, and come
To stand again, as in flesh, in a place

Of possibility. Unless there be
Within the figure of mortality
This mind of heaven whereby I may
Fashion the lips and be as breath again
In the mouth in which you were a word.

Or may the mind of heaven be a mind
Of questions? As: is there not a country
Or the negation of a country, where
The mortal tree where the bird sang, the season
Where you walked living, once existed only
In their own deaths before their tides and branches
Were from negation made? It is that world
That I would have wherein you might be loved,
And I would seek it in its own death, and shape
Its life out of your death, for it must be
Created out of the nothing that you are.

There must be found, then, the imagination
Before the names of things, the dicta for
The only poem, and among all dictions
That ceremony whereby you may be named
Perpetual out of the anonymity
Of death. I will make out of my grief
A river, and my rage shall be the coin
To catch its ferryman; out of my fear
A dog shall spring; I will fling my bitterness
To stop his throats. I will myself become
A Hades into which I can descend.

It will be a domain of déjà-vus,
The final most outlandish fastness of
Familiarity without memory,
Whose set dimensions, whose mode of privacy
And mode of pain I with my living breath
Shall enter, saying, "Like an Icarus
I have fallen into my shadow." There shall be seen

The death of the body walking in shapes of bodies,
Departure's self hid in a guise of sojourn,
As it seems among the living. But on those hills
The shadows of sheep are folded, not the sheep.

But on those lakes or the mirages of
Those lakes not birds are reflected, but the flight
Of birds across no sky. It is nevertheless
A place of recognition, though it be
Of recognition of nothing; a place of knowledge
Though it be knowledge of nothing; in this land
No landscape but a demeanor of distance
Where interchangeably the poles are death
And death, as in an opposition of mirrors
Where no beginning is, no end, I have lived
Not recognizing, for as long as knowledge.

Say it is the idea of a place
That has no imagination of its own;
Yet in these nothing-fertile notions of
Valleys, this static nature in a mind
Of motion were all motion and all mind
And the actual lake moving its metaphor
Under real birds conceived, although conceived
Only for uses elsewhere. It is between
These twin antinomies that I must walk
Casting, it seems, no image; between these poles
Of vanity that I must make you real.

And say that even here, this place that I
Make in a shadow, though I cast no image,
Make even as I walk here, there must be
In a kingdom of mirrors a king among
Mirrors, although he be no more
Than that image I do not cast: as it were
An ear upon the infinite silence, a something
Sovereign, before whom in some manner

I can stand to dispute his sovereignty
As before a mirror, saying, "Master of these
Echoing revels whose silence I violate . . ."

Or better, to a genius more alien there,
A deeper shadow more sorrowfully reposed,
Folded almost in memory, but sconced
In the necessity of that kingdom
As in an ancient throne, Persephone,
To say, "Oh Moon among such sanity,
Oh Other among the simulacra, Virgin
Madonna of the lap of sleep, conceiving
All flesh and holiness, I come to you calling,
Making you in a prayer, that your name
May know my voice and conceive a mercy."

Take it for answer when the hair lifts
There in no wind as in an insolence
Of wind: it is the self of highness in
That hollow, counterpart and partisan
Born of the argument, who listens. "Mistress,
I speak what you know: where the shadows were real
I loved a lady. Be not surprised
Now if I stand beyond lamentations, fictive
In places prepared for loss: save where she is
I am anomaly. Oh Name, what is her name
In anonymity, that I may call

And she be with me? For what is your Lord
Of Anonymity, Lord of Nothing
And Nowhere, if I know his name?
Unless he be also furtively somewhere
A lord of names? Mistress, what is your
Arrogant Chief Jack of Death but a hollow
Tale, my figment, nothing at all, unless
He be somewhere alive, alive? Tell him
That I who cast no shadow taunt him there

With the bogey of his name. How would he be
Death if I should imagine him otherwise?

Or rather, let me not be told her name
In death, for with such appellation
If I should call it would be in the attributes
Of death that she would come, and I am not used
To such reserves between us. But now, should I
Pronounce her as though she were alive,
Say it is a new word I make: not new
Merely for what the old words would not cover,
But an affirmation of what heretofore
Had not been so; let what has never been,
Suddenly, in terms of what is, be.

For I am instructed of this silence, Lady,
That what is not is of a nature
With what has never been; and Mention, though
It be the scholiast of memory,
Makes yet its presences from emptiness,
Speaks for the first time always, an improvisation,
Though in an ancient mode, a paradigm
For the unmentionable. Yet may the word
Be celebration of a permanence,
Make, so, a presence and a permanence,
The articulate dance, the turning festival."

"Creation," she says, "is your idea, then?"
"Lady, you know. Creation waits upon
The word; but you in silence are the conception
And the consent of speech, the metaphor
In the midst of chaos, whose word is love.
And though I would in her name shatter, drown
The clamorous dialectic of this silence
With irrefutable song, and though I had
Imagination to remove mountains

117

Out of their shadows, and did not have this love,
I were a vain instrument; I were nothing."

There in her shadow, voice in a gown of silence,
She says, "I, though I be the predicate
Of love, the image in the blather of death
To make that monotone intelligible
To itself, am yet this image in the blather
And terms of death, whose parlance will not be
By its own intelligibility gainsaid.
Creation," she says, "is perforce and always
The creation of a world, the world; it is
An infinite nature making infinite nature,
But death exacts therefor an infinite price.

What if, by uttering the terms of living
Upon this mortuary air, your head
Should become anomalous on your body
And neither be satisfied, but both walk, strange,
Fictive, among real familiars, or
Real but immortal among the figurative
But dying; or, undelighted by what fades,
Alien, unbelieving, unbelieved,
Live in a heart of celebration only?"
"If the terms stand, so be it. There in her
Living intimacy I am not foreign."

"There must be, before creation is,
A concept of beginnings, a notion
As of a rocking cradle not yet rocking
Where yet no cradle is: therein may time
The prodigy impossibly conceived
Upon itself, born of itself and still
Unborn, be laid, the sage, the quiet child
Conceiving timelessness." "I imagine
A song not temporal wherein may walk

The animals of time; I conceive a moment
In which time and that timelessness begin."

Creation is not raw, is not refined.
In a landscape of raw antecedent
Before belief, or a country refined
Beyond belief, without motion, without
Farewells, to which one does not say good-bye,
I, conceiving of creation, have
Conceived the novelty of farewell. I said,
"Let it be a time the sand whereof
May run somewhere besides away, may run
Nowhere perhaps at all. A time that lies
Immutable under eternal leaves."

And I therewith am already elsewhere
In a littoral not time's, though time has been
Godfather there and blessing, an ambit
As though of memory, but not memory's,
Where with a word I divide the literal
From the dead. Why should I notice the waters
Sundering from the waters, or suddenly
The first tree waving ancient fronds, or how
From novel shadows the new beasts come, the savage
Modulations of holiness, in love's name
Where other names are profanation?

For it is you that are the world thereof,
You whom, possessing, I have still desired,
And, touching, have still dreamed of; you the sense,
The echo there waiting upon this word,
The circle making all within it real,
The sole order; for I have painfully
Wrought you from vacancy to this full air
And sung you to the tender instrument
Of my ten fingers till you have become

The poem in whose arbor we may kiss,
The summer into which we can ascend.

You know the story, its dénouement. You know
Death is by definition a terrain
Of no return save to itself, where all
Appearances are voices calling, "Look
Now, oh look if now only"; is a face whereon
To look is to know loss; and what if I
Sould turn but once, and you vanish? The song is nothing
If not a resurrection. Therein I sing you,
Love, always more real, though in the fraying
Edges of patience the teased harpies
Hone the incredible silence against their tongues.

CANSO

I believe at dark solstice in the white moon sailing new;
And in my love, and in her hand, though the green shoot
    withered,
And in the twice-joining sea between us, and I believe
I lay long with the cold dead, although the word was summer,
The violent dead, and now
When the sun hangs in the low branches
Bleeding, and phoenix-like the white-feathered
Childish sibyl sings in the leaves of the dead year,
And northerly on another island
She smiles into the swirling mist, her trees
Half-sleeved in white, I believe
Resurrection stirs like the robin
Through the waters of the dead, and the buried blood,
Through the rain of two islands
To float like a lotus into the waking year
And stand wide-eyed like a lamb; I believe the dead
Mirrors of the sea shine soft with her new image always.

She is clear amber and the heaven's face
Seen under simple waters: there below
The lights, the vessels, the shore, the drift-shells stroking
The whipped weeds of the tide-race,
Under the fish flying and the laughter of her dolphins,
First cold, final echoes, and the salt dead, she is marine
And always the child among horses
At autumn by the dove-keep,
And the woman in tears in the green
Drowned wood in no time by the lost house on the slow
River, and always she is ancient as the sea's daughters,

As the green beginning; always the rites of her tides keen
Tender in my ears, her birds call me fair, her twining hands
Run gentle to my hands for honey, her lips bid me love
Her limbs in coral and the bursts of her dolphins
Always, the softness of her sea-changes
And the pride of her horses.

And there where the spume flies and the mews echoed and
    beckoned
The bowing drowned, because in her hands love and the one
    song
Leap and the long faith is born gladly, there through the
    waters
Of the dead, like the robin, singing, like the floating year,
The deep world in one island,
Streaming white from every dark-folded
Valley, till the green burgeons, and the long
Ghosts dripping leave the washed gold and the mounding joy,
The fruit swaying yellow, the shimmering birches
And the wise beaches lapped with the serpents and dead
Of the forgiving waters,
There, across green the gold light hanging,
The bees in the rosemary, the flashing pigeons,
Bud and harvest together,
The world in one island, because her hands are joy,
To no trumpet, all tongues singing the full silence,
Rises now and forever to gleam new as the white sea.

(Who sings now of the desperate seas, the bleak
Voyages by darkness, when the wind fell,
When the shadow waxed between us, and hails faded
And oar-sounds, when the last streak
Of the other lantern dwindled, and groped wakes, one by one
Ended in nothing, when separately we sailed seeking
By the four points and the foreign stars
Falling that may guide no man,
The treasure, the landfall, the morning,

122

Gray ease after night-fear, after shoal and cold swell
The harbor of one hand? Who sings, after the black whale-
    beds,
Tideless, and nautilus-marches, of the poles, the towers
Where we came each alone, of the widdershin wheels turning
By blue flames, where we lay dead in the grave's waters,
    though all
The world was summer? For the seven seas are one,
The four winds, and all journey and treasures
And islands, and the sung stars.)

Here is the gate of psalms, swordless, and the angel's country
For which we became as children; known earth and known
    heaven
Washed new in the ancient wonder; here in the high pastures,
Its roots in another story, offering innocence
Like apples, is the same tree;
Under the leaves and holy shadows
The same brightness springs where the stones begin
Laughter and green singing in the ancient rivers
And the new hours like the first shallows run;
There beyond pools and sheep bells where the dark browses
Already the gold pastures,
Are hushed grass and the bell of silence,
The silk-gray dusk, the mackerel sky for the moonrise,
Then the same moon riding new
Over the fields, the lulled falling of four rivers
And the praising hills and white leaves of paradise,
And swimming silver across her eyes and in the same sea.

Nightingales will sleep in the sycamores
Till there is no night; here will not the dark
Worm come with his sliding season, though the leaves fall,
Nor the snake in the small hours
Molest the young doves and thrushes with the snare of his
    hands
Nor sicken the drowsing fruit with the shadow of his tongue,

123

Nor chains nor temptations, till the end
Of time, nor any serpent,
Save the long tides, till the sea return.
She is clear amber, and the dawn found in the dark
By faith at last, by following sea-sounds, by the lost
Shells' singing, and like the sea she walks always beside me
Telling, and the warm deeps of her waters are never sung
Where, amid fathomless musics subtle beneath voices,
Softly she draws me down with her whispers and hands,
Her floods and eyes, face to face, telling me
Her white love, world without end.

Now, now I enter the first garden and the promised moon,
The silver of her thighs and shoulders; oh here where the
        sheaves
And shadows sway to her breath, in the caroling darkness
We embrace at last, and are night and morning together
And the gray-gold afternoon
Of marvels sinking over the hill
And the first and last tree; and all the leaves
Of our deaths are chanting, "Holy, holy, holy
Always were taper-light and ember-light,
Moon-light, the bowing stars, and that first glory still
Singing day from the darkness;
And never, save unto our amen
Shall the white sea surrender its dead, oh never,
Oh never. Amen. Amen."
We listen, and shall here, love, with the sea's holy
Song in the shells of our ears, lie down forever
To sleep in the turning garden for as long as the sea.

Green With Beasts

(1956)

TO DIDO

With dumb belongings there can be
The gesture that bestows, for its own reasons;
Its mumbled inadequacy reminds us always
In this world how little can be communicated.
And for these, they too are only tokens
Of what there is no word for: their worth
Is a breath or nothing, and the spirit who can convey?
I have doubts whether such things can be dedicated.
They themselves determine whose they are,
Announcing unbidden their conception
In a still place of perpetual surprise.
Can one offer things that know their own way
And will not be denied? These were bodied forth
In the country of your love: what other
Landscapes they may name, from that place
Is their language. In the cadences of that tongue
They learned what they are. How more can I make them
    yours?

LEVIATHAN

This is the black sea-brute bulling through wave-wrack,
Ancient as ocean's shifting hills, who in sea-toils
Travelling, who furrowing the salt acres
Heavily, his wake hoary behind him,
Shoulders spouting, the fist of his forehead
Over wastes gray-green crashing, among horses unbroken
From bellowing fields, past bone-wreck of vessels,
Tide-ruin, wash of lost bodies bobbing
No longer sought for, and islands of ice gleaming,
Who ravening the rank flood, wave-marshalling,
Overmastering the dark sea-marches, finds home
And harvest. Frightening to foolhardiest
Mariners, his size were difficult to describe:
The hulk of him is like hills heaving,
Dark, yet as crags of drift-ice, crowns cracking in thunder,
Like land's self by night black-looming, surf churning and trailing
Along his shores' rushing, shoal-water boding
About the dark of his jaws; and who should moor at his edge
And fare on afoot would find gates of no gardens,
But the hill of dark underfoot diving,
Closing overhead, the cold deep, and drowning.
He is called Leviathan, and named for rolling,
First created he was of all creatures,
He has held Jonah three days and nights,
He is that curling serpent that in ocean is,
Sea-fright he is, and the shadow under the earth.
Days there are, nonetheless, when he lies
Like an angel, although a lost angel
On the waste's unease, no eye of man moving,
Bird hovering, fish flashing, creature whatever

Who after him came to herit earth's emptiness.
Froth at flanks seething soothes to stillness,
Waits; with one eye he watches
Dark of night sinking last, with one eye dayrise
As at first over foaming pastures. He makes no cry
Though that light is a breath. The sea curling,
Star-climbed, wind-combed, cumbered with itself still
As at first it was, is the hand not yet contented
Of the Creator. And he waits for the world to begin.

BLUE COCKEREL

Morning was never here, nor more dark ever
Than now there is; but in the fixed green
And high branch of afternoon, this bird balances,
His blue feet splayed, folding nothing, as though
The too-small green limb were ground; and his shout
Frames all the silence. Not Montezuma nor all
The gold hills of the sun were ever so plumed
As the blue of his neck, his breast's orange, his wings'
Blazing, and the black-green sickles of his tail.
It seems to be summer. But save for his blue hackles
And the light haze of his back, there is no sky,
Only the one tree spreading its green flame
Like a new habit for heaven. It seems to be summer;
But on the single tree the fruits of all seasons
Hang in the hues of ripeness; but on the ground
The green is of spring, and the flowers
Of April are there. And he suspended, brilliant and foreign,
His wings as though beating the air of elsewhere,
Yet if he is not there, the rest is not either.
A cry must be painted silent: the spread red hand
Of his comb thrown back, beak wide, and the one eye
Glaring like the sun's self (for there is no other),
Like the sun seen small, seen rimmed in red secret,
May be the shape of jubilation crowing,
Or the stare and shriek of terror. And whose body
Is this in the foreground lying twisted sideways,
Eyes glazed, whose stiff posture would become
The contorted dead? Though its face gleams white
It might be the self of shadow we have not seen,
Night who was never here, or the hour itself

There to be sung unmoved. Surely it is
The eye's other centre, and upon this,
This only, the bird stares, and for this cause
Cries, cries, and his cry crashes
Among the branches, the blades of great leaves
Looming like towers, the fruits and petals, green
Thickets of light deeper than shadows, the moon-white
Ears of that body lying, and makes
And lends echo and moment to all that green
Watery silence. But does he scream
In joy unfading that now no dark is,
Or what wakening does he herald with all terror?

TWO HORSES

Oh in whose grove have we wakened, the bees
Still droning under the carved wall, the fountain playing
Softly to itself, and the gold light, muted,
Moving long over the olives; and whose,
Stamping the shadowy grass at the end of the garden,
Are these two wild horses tethered improbably
To the withes of a young quince? No rider
Is to be seen; they bear neither saddle nor bridle;
Their brute hooves splash the knee-high green
Without sound, and their flexed tails like flags float,
Whipping, their brows down like bulls. Yet the small tree
Is not shaken; and the broken arches
Of their necks in the dim air are silent
As the doorways of ruins. Birds flit in the garden:
Jay and oriole, blades in the hanging shadows,
Small cries confused. And dawn would be eastward
Over the dark neck a red mane tossed high
Like flame, and the dust brightening along the wall.
These have come up from Egypt, from the dawn countries,
Syria, and the land between the rivers,
Have ridden at the beaks of vessels, by Troy neighed,
And along the valley of the Danube, and to Etruria;
And all dust was of their making; and passion
Under their hooves puffed into flight like a sparrow
And died down when they departed. The haze of summer
Blows south over the garden terraces,
Vague through the afternoon, remembering rain;
But in the night green with beasts as April with grass
Orion would hunt high from southward, over the hill,
And the blood of beasts herald morning. Where these have passed,

131

Tramping white roads, their ears drinking the sword-crash,
The chariots are broken, bright battle-cars
Shambles under earth; whether by sharp bronze
Or the years' ebbing, all blood has flowed into the ground;
There was wailing at sundown, mourning for kings,
Weeping of widows, but these went faint, were forgotten,
And the columns have fallen like shadows. Crickets
Sing under the stones; and beyond the carved wall
Westward, fires drifting in darkness like the tails
Of jackals flaring, no hounds heard at their hunting,
Float outward into the dark. And these horses stamp
Before us now in this garden; and northward
Beyond the terraces the misted sea
Swirls endless, hooves of the gray wind forever
Thundering, churning the ragged spume-dusk
High that there be no horizons nor stars, and there
Are white islands riding, ghost-guarded, twisted waves flashing,
Porpoises plunging like the necks of horses.

DOG

He does not look fierce at all, propped scarcely erect
On skinny forelegs in the dust in the glare
In the dog-day heat, the small brown pariah at the edge
Of the shimmering vista of emptiness
Unbroken by any shade and seeming too permanent
To be of any day the afternoon.
Under the sky no colour or rather
The natural beige, dust-colour, merely
A brighter glare than the ground, beginning
Where the dust does not leave off, and rising
Through the shining distance that weighs and waves
Like water he does not have the air at all
Of vigilance: hindquarters collapsed
Under him like a rag lying shapeless
In the shrunk puddle of his shadow, coat
Caked and staring, hang-dog head
That his shoulders can hardly hold up from the dust
And from it dangling the faded tongue, the one
Colour to be seen. *Cave canem*; beware
The dog. But he squats harmless,
At his wildest, it might be, wishing that the feeble
Green cast the glare gives to his shadow
Could be green in truth, or be at least a wider
Shadow of some true green; and though he is
Free not tethered (but what in this place
Could one be free of if not the place) surely
He would never attack, nor move except perhaps,
Startled, to flee; surely those dirty tufts
Of coarse hair at his shoulders could never rise
Hostile in hackles, and he has forgotten

133

Long since the wish to growl; or if he should bare
His teeth it would not be with a lifting
Of lips but with a letting-fall, as it is
With the grins of the dead. And indeed what is there here
That he might keep watch over? The dust? The empty
Distance, the insufferable light losing itself
In its own glare? Whatever he was to guard
Is gone. Besides, his glazed eyes
Fixed heavily ahead stare beyond you
Noticing nothing; he does not see you. But wrong:
Look again: it is through you
That he looks, and the danger of his eyes
Is that in them you are not there. He guards indeed
What is gone, what is gone, what has left not so much
As a bone before him, which vigilance needs
No fierceness, and his weariness is not
From the length of his watch, which is endless,
But because nothing, not the weight of days
Not hope, the canicular heat, the dust, nor the mortal
Sky, is to be borne. Approach
If you dare, but doing so you take
In your hands what life is yours, which is less
Than you suppose, for he guards all that is gone,
And even the shimmer of the heated present,
Of the moment before him in which you stand
Is a ghost's shimmer, its past gone out of it, biding
But momently his vigil. Walk past him
If you please, unmolested, but behind his eyes
You will be seen not to be there, in the glaring
Uncharactered reaches of oblivion, and guarded
With the rest of vacancy. Better turn from him
Now when you can and pray that the dust you stand in
And your other darlings be delivered
From the vain distance he is the power of.

WHITE GOAT, WHITE RAM

The gaiety of three winds is a game of green
Shining, of grey-and-gold play in the holly-bush
Among the rocks on the hill-side, and if ever
The earth was shaken, say a moment ago
Or whenever it came to be, only the leaves and the spread
Sea still betray it, trembling; and their tale betides
The faintest of small voices, almost still.
A road winds among the grey rocks, over the hill,
Arrives from out of sight, from nowhere we know,
Of an uncertain colour; and she stands at the side
Nearer the sea, not far from the brink, legs straddled wide
Over the swinging udder, her back and belly
Slung like a camp of hammocks, her head raised,
The narrow jaw grinding sideways, ears flapping sideways,
Eyes wide apart like the two moons of Mars
At their opposing. So broadly is she blind
Who has no names to see with: over her shoulder
She sees not summer, not the idea of summer,
But green meanings, shadows, the gold light of now, familiar,
The sense of long day-warmth, of sparse grass in the open
Game of the winds; an air that is plenitude,
Describing itself in no name; all known before,
Perceived many times before, yet not
Remembered, or at most felt as usual. Even the kids,
Grown now and gone, are forgotten,
As though by habit. And he on the other side
Of the road, hooves braced among spurge and asphodel,
Tears the grey grass at its roots, his massive horns
Tossing delicately, as by long habit, as by

Habit learned, or without other knowledge
And without question inherited, or found
As first he found the air, the first daylight, first milk at the tetter,
The paths, the pen, the seasons. They are white, these two,
As we should say those are white who remember nothing,
And we for our uses call that innocence,
So that our gracelessness may have the back of a goat
To ride away upon; so that when our supreme gesture
Of propitiation has obediently been raised
It may be the thicket-snared ram that dies instead of the son;
So even that we may frame the sense that is now
Into a starred figure of last things, of our own
End, and there by these beasts know ourselves
One from another: some to stay in the safety
Of the rock, but many on the other hand
To be dashed over the perilous brink. There is no need
Even that they should be gentle, for us to use them
To signify gentleness, for us to lift them as a sign
Invoking gentleness, conjuring by their shapes
The shape of our desire, which without them would remain
Without a form and nameless. For our uses
Also are a dumbness, a mystery,
Which like a habit stretches ahead of us
And was here before us; so, again, we use these
To designate what was before us, since we cannot
See it in itself, for who can recognize
And call by true names, familiarly, the place
Where before this he was, though for nine months
Or the world's full age he housed there? Yet it seems
That by such a road, arriving from out of sight,
From nowhere we know, we may have come, and these
Figure as shapes we may have been. Only, to them
The road is less than a road, though it divides them,
A bit of flat space merely, perhaps not even
A thing that leads elsewhere, except when they
Are driven along it, for direction is to them
The paths their own preference and kinds have made

And follow: routes through no convenience
And world of ours, but through their own sense
And mystery. Mark this; for though they assume
Now the awkward postures of illustrations
For all our parables, yet the mystery they stand in
Is still as far from what they signify
As from the mystery we stand in. It is the sign
We make of them, not they, that speaks from their dumbness
That our dumbness may speak. There in the thin grass
A few feet away they browse beyond words; for a mystery
Is that for which we have not yet received
Or made the name, the terms, that may enclose
And call it. And by virtue of such we stand beyond
Earthquake and wind and burning, and all the uncovenanted
Terror of becoming, and beyond the small voice; and on
Another hand, as it were a little above us
There are the angels. We are dumb before them, and move
In a different mystery; but may there be
Another road we do not see as a road: straight, narrow,
Or broad or the sector of a circle, or perhaps
All these, where without knowing it we stand
On one side or another? I have known such a way
But at moments only, and when it seemed I was driven
Along it, and along no other that my preference
Or kind had made. And of these others above us
We know only the whisper of an elusive sense,
Infrequent meanings and shadows, analogies
With light and the beating of wings. Yet now, perhaps only
A few feet away in the shaking leaves they wait
Beyond our words, beyond earthquake, whirlwind, fire,
And all the uncovenanted terror of becoming,
And beyond the small voice. Oh we cannot know and we are not
What we signify, but in what sign
May we be innocent, for out of our dumbness
We would speak for them, give speech to the mute tongues
Of angels. Listen: more than the sea's thunder
Foregathers in the grey cliffs; the roots of our hair

137

Stir like the leaves of the holly bush where now
Not games the wind ponders, but impatient
Glories, fire: and we go stricken suddenly
Humble, and the covering of our feet
Offends, for the ground where we find we stand is holy.

PART TWO

THE BATHERS

They make in the twining tide the motions of birds.
Such are the cries, also, they exchange
In their nakedness that is soft as a bird's
Held in the hand, and as fragile and strange.

And the blue mirror entertains them till they take
The sea for another bird: the crumbling
Hush-hush where the gentlest of waves break
About their voices would be his bright feathers blowing.

Only the dull shore refrains. But from this patient
Bird each, in the plumage of his choice,
Might learn the deep shapes and secret of flight

And the shore be merely a perch to which they might
Return. And the mirror turns serpent
And their only sun is swallowed up like a voice.

THE WILDERNESS

Remoteness is its own secret. Not holiness,
Though, nor the huge spirit miraculously avoiding
The way's dissemblings, and undue distraction or drowning
At the watercourses, has found us this place,

But merely surviving all that is not here,
Till the moment that looks up, almost by chance, and sees
Perhaps hands, feet, but not ourselves; a few stunted juniper
     trees
And the horizon's virginity. We are where we always were.

The secret becomes no less itself for our presence
In the midst of it; as the lizard's gold-eyed
Mystery is no more lucid for being near.

And famine is all about us, but not here;
For from the very hunger to look, we feed
Unawares, as at the beaks of ravens.

THE WAKENING

Looking up at last from the first sleep
Of necessity rather than of pure delight
While his dreams still rode and lapped like the morning light
That everywhere in the world shimmered and lay deep

So that his sight was half dimmed with its dazzling, he could see
Her standing naked in the day-shallows there,
Face turned away, hands lost in her bright hair;
And he saw then that her shadow was the tree:

For in a place where he could never come
Only its darkness underlay the day's splendour,
So that even as she stood there it must reach down

Through not roots but branches with dark bird-song, into a
    stream
Of silence like a sky but deeper
Than this light or than any remembered heaven.

THE PRODIGAL SON

for Leueen MacGrath Kaufman

I

Except for the flies, except that there is not water
Enough for miles to make a mirror, the face
Of the afternoon might seem an empty lake,
Still, shining, burnished beyond the semblance
Of water until the semblance of afternoon
Was all the surface that shimmered there, even
The dust shining and hanging still, the dusty
Carob trees and olives gleaming, all hung
Untouchable and perfect, as in its own
Mirage. Or else the afternoon, the shapes
So still in the heat, and burnished, in such intensity
Of shining stillness, seem other than themselves,
Seem fragments and faces half-seen through their own
Glare, shaping another life, another
Lifelessness that mirrors this as might
Its own mirage. Except for the flies. There
Where the far hills seem the sheen of a dusty hanging
Hovering like a breath just out of reach
The slack tents of the herders lean, and the flocks
Lie motionless under the trees, the men
Not moving, lying among them. And between
There and the ruled shade of this white wall
There is nothing: distance is dead, unless
It is in distance that the flies hum.

II

And the silence off on the hills might be an echo
Of the silence here in the shadow of the white wall
Where the old man sits brooding upon distance
Upon emptiness. His house behind him,
The white roofs flat and domed, hushed with the heat
And the hour, and making what it can of shadow
While no one stirs, is it in fact the same
In which lifelong he has believed and filled
With life, almost as a larger body, or is it,
Now suddenly in this moment between mirage
And afternoon, another, and farther off
Than the herdsmen, oh much farther, its walls glaring
White out of a different distance, deceiving
By seeming familiar, but an image merely
By which he may know the face of emptiness,
A name with which to say emptiness? Yet it is the same
Where he performs as ever the day's labour,
The gestures of pleasure, as is necessary,
Speaks in the name of order, and is obeyed
Among his sons, except one, except the one
Who took his portion and went. There is no distance
Between himself now and emptiness; he has followed
The departing image of a son beyond
Distance into emptiness. The flies crawl
Unnoticed over his face, through his drooping
Beard, along his hands lying loose as his beard,
Lying in his lap like drying leaves; and before him
The smeared stalls of the beasts, the hens in the shade,
The water-crane still at the well-head, the parched
Fields that are his as far as the herdsmen
Are emptiness in his vacant eyes.

III

But distance,
He remembers, was not born at a son's departure
Nor died with his disappearance; and he recognizes
That emptiness had lodged with him before,
Lived with him in fact always, but humbly,
In corners, under different names, showing
Its face but seldom, and then had been for the most part
Ignored. And now at the loss of one son
Only when all else remains, not fearful
For the sake of what remains, but for the love, simply,
Of what is lost (unto this has been likened
The kingdom of heaven) he sits in the afternoon
Of vacancy, by licence of vacancy,
For emptiness is lord of his hollow house,
Sits at his side at table, devouring,
Shows him from room to room, for all faces
Of loss, the known and the foreboded, all
Figments of fear and grieving, the new
And the remembered, are swollen and grown
To insolent possession there, feed
At home on all the limbs of his life, fix and focus
Their image there on the dying in distance
Of distance, on dying by distances,
On that one departure, as on the empty frame
Of the door the son went out by.

IV

                              He went out by that door
Eagerly, not lingering to look back,
Bearing with him all that could be carried
Of his inheritance, since he was of an age
To take what was his and leave, and his father
Gave him his portion, who would not willingly
Have had him lack for anything, not even
For the distance beyond his doors. He went out
Looking for something his father had not given,
Delights abroad, some foreign ease, something
Vague because distant, which he must give
Himself, something indeed which he carried,
Unknowing, already with him; or, say, an ampler
Body, an assured content, something
Which, unknowing, he was leaving behind, yet
Which he had to leave to be able to find. And wasted
His substance in wild experiment and found
Emptiness only, found nothing in distance,
Sits finally in a sty and broods
Upon emptiness, upon distance.
                              Except
For the flies hovering and crawling before
His eyes, insisting that the afternoon
He sees is there, the dusty grass, the unholy
Swine, the shared husks, the shared hut shining
Like brass in the oddest places might be a mirage
Merely in which he had no part, a strange
Vista made of familiar pieces caught
In an odd light in a mirror, an image
Of emptiness out of a restive day-dream
Gone wrong at home; unreal, if he could turn
The mirror, open his eyes. And all between
This hour and corner where he sits and his father's
Door that day when he walked away, surely
Is unreal, a picture in which he has no part,

Leading to this—the loud junketings, the women,
The silks, columns, the intricate pleasure
Of generosity; his mind turns among
Those vacancies as a mirror hung by a string
In a ruin. Distance might be dead
Except for the flies, and instead of the emptiness
On which he stares, the backs of the sleeping swine
Might be the far hills beyond the hens,
Beyond the hushed water-crane and the fields
By his father's house; the shade where he sits
Be the ruled shadow of the white wall, or at least
He might be lying just out of reach under
A tree among the herders; oh except
For the flies' insistence, the sty must be
A heap of ashes, and the swineherd's fouled garment
Sackcloth.

V

So in the empty frame of an old man's
Mind the figments of afternoon
Wait between a substance that is not theirs
And an illusion that is another's: the herders
Wait on the hills, the dusty olives, the fields,
Well-crane and white walls are a held
Breath waiting; and the dozing calf
Fattens and waits, the other sons asleep
With their wives in complacent dreams
Wait in emptiness and do not know
That it is emptiness, that they are waiting,
That the flies are wrong and hover in nothing,
That distance is dead, that in the same mirage
Nearer than the flies or the herders, the lost son,
Hesitant, stumbling among the swine (unto this
Has been likened the kingdom of heaven) hoping
For little, takes the first step toward home.

THE ANNUNCIATION

It was not night, not even when the darkness came
That came blacker than any night, and more fearful,
Like a bell beating and I under its darkness dying
To the stun of the sound. Before that
It was not dark nor loud nor any way strange,
Just the empty kitchen, with the smell of the bean-flowers
In their late blossom, coming in at the window,
And the stillness, just that empty hour of the afternoon
     When it is hard indeed to believe in time.

When the young grass sleeps white in the sun, and the tree's
  shadow
Lies so still on the small stone by the doorway
You would think the stone was only a shadow
Rounded, and nothing beneath, and the air
Forgets to move, forgets, and you can hear a humming,
It is like a humming, but it is not a sound
But the edges of the silence whirring
To tell you how deep the silence is. When, even
Though it is spring, and the coldness of winter
And the coldness of morning still under the air,
If you do not think, you can feel already
The turned summer, the daze, the dryness,
     The light heavy in the air.

So that time is hard to believe, but it is with you
More than ever, for you can feel the stillness
Rushing more sudden than ever, in the open day
More secret than ever, and farther and harder
To understand, and all so still. And I was thinking

Can it be true, like the stone under the shadow;
Can it be true? And thinking how they tell
That a woman is for a man, and that from a man
She learns many things and can make names for them
That, before, she was empty of. And of this man
That will take me as a woman, and he is a good man.
And yet thinking how men and women, even
Together in their understanding, are lost
In that secret, and the names they made. And sometimes
You can stand in that emptiness till you are thinking
Of nothing, and it sounds as though a kind
Of joy began whirring at the edge of that sadness,
Like a sudden peace that was there, but it is not whirring
It is so still, but you are drawn out on it
Till you are as empty as the hushed hour,
              And there is no word for it all.

That was the way it was, and in the fragrant light
That came in at the window, I was standing
Still, that way, seeing nothing but the light,
As though I was gliding out on the peaceful light
Like water; and what I was, in myself
I was nothing. And had even forgotten whatever
I should have been doing; only in my two hands
I was holding a cup, I remember, the kind
You would measure flour or drink water in,
But wherever I was going with it, and why,
I had stopped and forgotten, because of the secret
Way of the stillness, and myself, and the light,
So that now, the reason why I was holding
That cup in my hands is one of the things I cannot
              Remember nor understand.

Then the darkness began: it brushed
Just lightly first, like it might be the wing
Of a bird, a soft bird, that flutters,
As it comes down. It brushed the hem of the light

And in my eyes, where I was nothing. But grew
Clouding between my eyes and the light
And rushing upon me, the way the shadow
Of a cloud will rush over the sunned fields
In a time of wind; and the black coming down
In its greatness, between my eyes and the light,
Was like wings growing, and the blackness
Of their shadow growing as they came down
Whirring and beating, cold and like thunder, until
All the light was gone, and only that noise
And terrible darkness, making everything shake
Like the end of it was come, and there was
No word for it, and I thought Lord, Lord, and thought
How if I had not gone out on the light
And been hidden away on the vanished light
So that myself I was empty and nothing
I would surely have died, because the thing
That the darkness was, and the wings and the shaking
That there was no word for it, was a thing that in myself
I could not have borne and lived. And still came
Nearer and darker, beating, and there was
Like a whisper in the feathers there, in the wings'
Great wind, like a whirring of words, but I could not
Say the shape of them, and it came to me .
They were like a man, but none has yet come to me,
And I could not say how. Only, in the place
Where, myself, I was nothing, there was suddenly
A great burning under the darkness, a fire
Like fighting up into the wings' lash and the beating
Blackness, and flames like the tearing of teeth,
With noise like rocks rending, such that no word
Can call it as it was there, and for fire only,
Without the darkness beating and the wind, had I
Been there, had I not been far on the hiding light
I could not have borne it and lived. And then the stillness:
The wings giving way all at once, and the fire quiet
Leaving neither day nor darkness, but only the silence

149

That closed like a last clap of the thunder
And was perfect. And the light lying beyond, like a ring,
And the things in it lying, and everything still
With no moving at all, and no pulse, nor any breath,
And no rushing in that stillness, for time was not there,
Nor the emptiness, the way time falls into emptiness,
But only fullness, like it was forever,
Like it was everything from the beginning and always,
In itself and still, and not even waiting,
Because it was there. And in the silence
And in the fullness it came, it was there
Like it had not come but was there, whatever it was
That above all I cannot name.

Though in itself it was like a word, and it was
Like no man and no word that ever was known,
Come where I was; and because I was nothing
It could be there. It was a word for
The way the light and the things in the light
Were looking into the darkness, and the darkness
And the things of the darkness were looking into the light
In the fullness, and the way the silence
Was hearing, like it was hearing a great song
And the song was hearing the silence forever
And forever and ever. And I knew the name for it;
There in the place where I was nothing in
The fullness, I knew it, and held it and knew
The way of it, and the word for how it was one,
I held it, and the word for why. Or almost,
Or believed I knew it, believed, like an echo
That when it comes you believe you know
The word, while it rings, but when it is gone
You had not learned it, and cannot find it, even
Though the sound still breathes in your ear. Because
Then the light looked away from the darkness
Again, and the song slid into the silence
And was lost again, and the fullness rose, going,

And the sound of its going was the sound of wings
Rushing away in darkness, and the sound
That came after them was the stillness rushing
Again, and time sudden and hard to believe,
And forever was emptiness again, where time fell,
And I was standing there in myself, in the light,
With only the shape of the word that is wonder,
                    And that same cup still in my hands.

And I could not say how long it had been
That I had stood there forever, while the end
Looked into the beginning, and they were one
And the word for one. Because the shadow
Had not changed on the stone, and nothing had moved
In all that time, if it was in time at all,
Because nothing had changed. But I did not doubt
For the wonder that was in me, quickening,
Like in your ear the shape of a sound
When the sound is gone. And because when
At last I moved my hand, slowly, slowly,
Like it could not believe, to touch myself, to see
If it could be true, if I had truly come back
From the light, and touched myself like something
Hard to believe, I knew I was not the same
And could not say how. Then a long time I stood there
Pondering the way of it in my heart, and how
                    The coming of it was a blessing.

Afterwards, though, there was the emptiness
And not as it was before: not drifting
About the place where I stood, like the afternoon
Light and the smell of the bean-flowers, but as though
There was emptiness only, and the great falling
And nothing besides, and it was all inside me
In the place where I had been nothing: the stillness
Rushing, and time not hard to believe then
But undeniable in the pain of its falling,

And the darkness where time fell and men and women
Together in their understanding, and the names
That they made and everything from the beginning
Like they were falling inside me, in the emptiness
That I was, and because of me they were falling,
Because I had been nothing. So that I thought then
That that was the change I had known, the only change,
But yet I would not believe that, but I cannot
Say why. And so that I would have prayed
That it be removed from me, the grief of it,
The keen that was in me at all their falling
In the emptiness that I was be removed from me,
But then how should I have named it, and what am I
That He should be mindful of? But I prayed,
But for that I did not pray, but yet I
Cannot say why, but in my heart that also
I pondered. And it went when its time was,
Because in the place where we are, the shadow
Moves and there is the stone again, and the day
Going and things to be done, the same
As always, the way they have to be; and because
Such emptiness as that was, you could not
Bear it for long and live, or I could not.
So I moved away about something
That all that time I should have been doing, with
That cup in my hands; whatever it was
                    I have forgotten again.

And I moved away because you must live
Forward, which is away from whatever
It was that you had, though you think when you have it
That it will stay with you forever. Like that word
I thought I had known and held surely and that it
Was with me always. In the evening
Between the shadows the light lifts and slides
Out and out, and the cold that was under the air
Is the darkness you remember, and how it was

There all the time and you had forgotten.
It carries its own fragrance. And there is this man
Will take me as a woman, and he is a good man,
And I will learn what I am, and the new names. Only
If I could remember, if I could only remember
The way that word was, and the sound of it. Because
There is that in me still that draws all that I am
Backwards, as weeds are drawn down when the water
Flows away; and if I could only shape
And hear again that word and the way of it—
But you must grow forward, and I know
That I cannot. And yet it is there in me:
As though if I could only remember
The word, if I could make it with my breath
It would be with me forever as it was
Then in the beginning, when it was
The end and the beginning, and the way
They were one; and time and the things of falling
Would not fall into emptiness but into
The light, and the word tell the way of their falling
Into the light forever, if I could remember
                And make the word with my breath.

THE MOUNTAIN

Only on the rarest occasions, when the blue air,
Though clear, is not too blinding (as, say,
For a particular moment just at dusk in autumn)
Or if the clouds should part suddenly
Between freshets in spring, can one trace the rising
Slopes high enough to call them contours; and even
More rarely see above the treeline. Then
It is with almost a shock that one recognizes
What supposedly one had known always:
That it is, in fact, a mountain; not merely
This restrictive sense of nothing level, of never
Being able to go anywhere
But up or down, until it seems probable
Sometimes that the slope, to be so elusive
And yet so inescapable, must be nothing
But ourselves: that we have grown with one
Foot shorter than the other, and would deform
The levellest habitat to our misshapen
Condition, as is said of certain hill creatures.

Standing between two other peaks, but not
As they: or so we have seen in a picture
Whose naive audacity, founded as far as can be
Determined, on nothing but the needs
Of its own composition, presents all three
As shaped oddly, of different colours, rising
From a plain whose flatness appears incredible
To such as we. Of course to each of us
Privately, its chief difference from its peers
Rests not even in its centrality, but its

Strangeness composed of our own intimacy
With a part of it, our necessary
Ignorance of its limits, and diurnal pretence
That what we see of it is all. Learned opinions differ
As to whether it was ever actively
Volcanic. It is believed that if one could see it
Whole, its shape might make this clearer, but that
Is impossible, for at the distance at which in theory
One could see it all, it would be out of sight.

Of course in all the senses in which any
Place or thing can be said not to exist
Until someone, at least, is known to have been there,
It would help immeasurably if anyone
Should ever manage to climb it. No one,
From whatever distance, has ever so much as seen
The summit, or even anywhere near it; not, that is,
As far as we know. At one time the attempt
Was a kind of holy maelstrom, Mecca
For fanatics and madmen, and a mode of ritual
And profane suicide (since among us there is nowhere
From which one could throw oneself down). But there have been
Expeditions even quite recently, and with the benefit
Of the most expensive equipment. Very few
Who set out at all seriously have
Come back. At a relatively slight distance
Above us, apparently the whole aspect and condition
Of the mountain changes completely; there is ceaseless wind
With a noise like thunder and the beating of wings.

Indeed, if one considers the proximity
Of the point at which so much violence
Is known to begin, it is not our failure
That strikes one as surprising, but our impunity:
The summer camps on near gradients, ski-lifts in winter,
And even our presence where we are. For of those
Who attained any distance and returned, most

Were deafened, some permanently; some were blind,
And these also often incurably; all
Without exception were dazzled, as by a great light. And those
Who perhaps went furthest and came back, seemed
To have completely lost the use of our language,
Or if they spoke, babbled incoherently
Of silence bursting beyond that clamour, of time
Passed there not passing here, which we could not understand,
Of time no time at all. These characteristic
Effects of the upper slopes—especially the derangement
Of time-sense, and the dazzling—seem from earliest
Antiquity to have excited speculation.

One legend has it that a remote king-priest figure
Once gained the summit, spent some—to him non-sequent
But to them significant—time there, and returned
'Shining', bearing ciphers of the arcane (which,
Translated into the common parlance, proved
To be a list of tribal taboos) like clastic
Specimens, and behaved with a glacial violence
Later construed as wisdom. This, though
Charming, does not, in the light of current endeavour,
Seem possible, even though so long ago. Yet
To corroborate this story, in the torrent
Gold has been found which even at this
Late date appears to have been powdered by hand,
And (further to confuse inquiry) several
Pediments besides, each with four sockets shaped
As though to receive the hoof of a giant statue
Of some two-toed ungulate. Legend being
What it is, there are those who still insist
He will come down again some day from the mountain.

As there are those who say it will fall on us. It
Will fall. And those who say it has already
Fallen. It has already fallen. Have we not
Seen it fall in shadow, evening after evening,

Across everything we can touch; do we not build
Our houses out of the great hard monoliths
That have crashed down from far above us? Shadows
Are not without substance, remind and predict;
And we know we live between greater commotions
Than any we can describe. But, most important:
Since this, though we know so little of it, is
All we know, is it not whatever it makes us
Believe of it—even the old woman
Who laughs, pointing, and says that the clouds across
Its face are wings of seraphim? Even the young
Man who, standing on it, declares it is not
There at all. He stands with one leg habitually
Bent, to keep from falling, as though he had grown
That way, as is said of certain hill creatures.

SAINT SEBASTIAN

So many times I have felt them come, Lord,
The arrows (a coward dies often), so many times,
And worse, oh worse often than this. Neither breeze nor bird
Stirring the hazed peace through which the day climbs.

And slower even than the arrows, the few sounds that come
Falling, as across water, from where farther off than the hills
The archers move in a different world in the same
Kingdom. Oh, can the noise of angels,

The beat and whirring between Thy kingdoms
Be even by such cropped feathers raised? Not though
With the wings of the morning may I fly from Thee; for it is

Thy kingdom where (and the wind so still now)
I stand in pain; and, entered with pain as always,
Thy kingdom that on these erring shafts comes.

THE ISAIAH OF SOUILLAC

Why the prophet is dancing the sculptor knew. If
The prophet is dancing. Or even if it is only
Wind, a wind risen there in the doorway
Suddenly as a fish leaps, lifting his garments
His feet, like music, a whirling of breath carved
There in the narrow place that is enough for a man.
You see a wind in its signs but in itself not.
You hear a spirit in its motion, in its words, even
In its stillness, but in itself not. Know it here in the stance
Of a prophet, and his beard blown in a doorway.
His words stream in the stoney wind; woe
Unto the dust that is deaf, for even stones
Can rise as with feet when the spirit passes
Upon the place where they are. But they are all gone away
Backward; from the soles of their feet to their heedless heads
There is no measure nor soundness in them. His fingers,
Frail as reeds making the music they move to,
Embody a lightness like fire. They shall be moved
With burning whom this breath moves not, who have refused
The waters of Shiloah that go softly shall the river
Rise over, out in the sunlight, roaring
Like the sea, like lions, spreading its wings like a wind.
And yet will the wind of heaven wear the shape of a man,
Be mortal as breath, before men, for a sign, and stand
Between good and evil, the thieves of the left and right hand.
And the sign of a wind is dancing, the motion
Of a sign is dancing and ushered with words beating
And with dancing. So there is terrible gentleness
Unleashed in the stone of his eyes, so
The words dance as a fire, as a clapping

Of hands, as the stars dance, as the mountains
Leap swelling, as the feet of the prophet, faithful
Upon them, dance, dance, and still to the same song.

THE STATION

Two boards with a token roof, backed
Against the shelving hill, and a curtain
Of frayed sacking which the wind absently
Toyed with on the side toward the sea:
From that point already so remote that we
Continually caught ourselves talking in whispers
No path went on but only the still country
Unfolding as far as we could see
In the luminous dusk its land that had not been lived on
Ever, or not within living memory.

This less than shelter, then, was the last
Human contrivance for our encouragement:
Improvised so hastily, it might have been
Thrown together only the moment
Before we arrived, yet so weathered,
Warped and parched, it must have stood there
Longer than we knew. And the ground before it
Was not scarred with the rawness of construction
Nor even beaten down by feet, but simply barren
As one felt it always had been: something between
Sand and red shale with only the spiky dune-grass
Growing, and a few trees stunted by wind.

Some as they arrived appeared to be carrying
Whole households strapped onto their shoulders,
Often with their tired children asleep
Among the upper baskets, and even
A sore dog limping behind them. Some
Were travelling light for the journey:

A knife and matches, and would sleep
In the clothes they stood up in. And there were
The barefoot ones, some from conviction
With staves, some from poverty with nothing.

Burdens and garments bore no relation
To the ages of the travellers; nor, as they sat
In spite of fatigue talking late
Into the night, to the scope and firmness
Of their intentions. It was, for example,
A patriarch herding six grandchildren
In his family, and who had carried
More than his own weight of gear all day
Who insisted that three days' journey inland
Would bring them to a sheltered valley
Along a slow river, where even the clumsiest farmer
Would grow fat on the land's three crops a year.

And a youth with expensive hiking shoes
And one blanket to carry, who declaimed
Most loudly on the effort of the trip,
The stingy prospects, the risks involved
In venturing beyond that point. Several
Who had intended to go furthest mused
That the land thereabouts was better
Than what they had left and that tramping
Behind his own plough should be far enough afield
For any grown man, while another, to all
Dissuasions repeated that it had been
The same ten years ago at — naming a place
Where we had slept two nights before.
Until one who looked most energetic
Changed the subject with his theory
That a certain block of stone there
Before the doorway had been shaped
By hand, and at one time had stood
As the pedestal of a wayside shrine.

Yet in spite of the circling arguments
Which grew desperate several times before morning
Everyone knew that it was all decided:
That some, even who spoke with most eloquence
Of the glories of exodus and the country
Waiting to be taken, would be found
Scrabbling next day for the patch of ground
Nearest the shelter, or sneaking back
The way they had come, or hiring themselves out
As guides to this point, and no one would be able
To explain what had stopped them there; any more
Than one would be able afterwards to say
Why some who perhaps sat there saying least,
And not, to appearances, the bravest
Or best suited for such a journey,
At first light would get up and go on.

THE MASTER

Not entirely enviable, however envied;
And early outgrew the enjoyment of their envy,
For othe r preoccupations, some quite as absurd.
Not always edifying in his action: touchy
And dull by turns, prejudiced, often not strictly
Truthful, with a weakness for petty meddling,
For black sheep, churlish rancours, and out-of-hand damning.

The messes he got himself into were of his own devising.
He had all the faults he saw through in the rest of us;
As we have taken pains, and a certain delight, in proving,
Not denying his strength, but still not sure quite where it was;
But luck was with him too, whatever that is,
For his rightful deserts, far from destroying him,
Turned out to be just what he'd needed, and he used them.

Opportunist, shrewd waster, half calculation,
Half difficult child; a phoney, it would seem
Even to his despairs, were it not for the work, and that certain
Sporadic but frightening honesty allowed him
By those who loathed him most. Not nice in the home,
But a few loved him. And he loved. Who? What? Some still
Think they know, as some thought they knew then, which is just
    as well.

In his lifetime what most astonished those
Acquainted with him, was the amount of common
Detail he could muster, and with what intimate ease,
As though he knew it all from inside. For when
Had he seen it? They recalled him as one who most often

Seemed slow, even stupid, not above such things surely,
But absent, with that air maybe part fake, and part shifty.

Yet famously cursed in his disciples:
So many, emulous, but without his unique powers,
Could only ape and exaggerate his foibles.
And he bewildered them as he did no others,
Though they tried to conceal it: for, like mirrors
In a fun-house, they were static, could never keep up with him,
Let alone predict. But stranded on strange shores following him.

So the relief, then the wide despair, when he was gone;
For not only his imitators did he leave feeling
Naked, without voice or manner of their own:
For over a generation his ghost would come bullying
Every hand: all modes seemed exhausted, and he had left nothing
Of any importance for them to do,
While what had escaped him eluded them also.

For only with his eyes could they see, with his ears hear
The world. He had made it. And hard, now, to believe
In the invention: all seems so styleless, as though it had come there
By itself, since the errors and effort are in their grave.
But real: here we are walking in it. Oh what we can never forgive
Is the way every leaf calls up to our helpless remembrance
Our reality and its insupportable innocence.

TOBACCO

'Nothing in the world like it; you can tell Aristotle.'
And a filthy habit too; yet the ghost of this burning,
Imbibed with practice, is balm undeniable,
So rejoicing the senses, so pleasant to the tongue,
That once they know it, they crave it still. Which, faking
With pencil shavings, in a pipe where the soap still bubbled,
I would pretend I was addicted to, as a child.

Grows faster than you would believe, once it gets going.
The devil green in it. And lovely
The big leaves, in the least air wagging and slatting
Like hands strung up loose at the wrists, or heads vacantly
Disapproving; but if we are made that way
It is lunacy, surely, to carp at nature
Especially when there is so much to enjoy in her.

To avoid the tax on it (we will soon
Be assessed for breathing) if you have even one green finger
The weed will flourish in your own garden
—Hoe often: the roots like access to God's sweet air—
Though the result may prove rather more rank than you prefer
If the cure of it is dependent on just your own
Crude devices: the drying, the disguising of the poison.

Oh yes, a vice. You knew it beforehand. And you
Would give it up, normally, but it's a help when you're working.
You can keep it within reason. Just the same, it will kill you
In the end: you can feel it now tarring
Your lungs to a shameful squeak, feel your heart constricting;
But as you bemoan it in horrified amaze
At how much it costs, think too what fun it is.

BURNING THE CAT

In the spring, by the big shuck-pile
Between the bramble-choked brook where the copperheads
Curled in the first sun, and the mud road,
All at once it could no longer be ignored.
The season steamed with an odour for which
There has never been a name, but it shouted above all.
When I went near, the wood-lice were in its eyes
And a nest of beetles in the white fur of its arm-pit.
I built a fire there by the shuck-pile
But it did no more than pop the beetles
And singe the damp fur, raising a stench
Of burning hair that bit through the sweet day-smell.
Then thinking how time leches after indecency,
Since both grief is indecent and the lack of it,
I went away and fetched newspaper,
And wrapped it in dead events, days and days,
Soaked it in kerosene and put it in
With the garbage on a heaped nest of sticks:
It was harder to burn than the peels of oranges,
Bubbling and spitting, and the reek was like
Rank cooking that drifted with the smoke out
Through the budding woods and clouded the shining dogwood.
But I became stubborn: I would consume it
Though the pyre should take me a day to build
And the flames rise over the house. And hours I fed
That burning, till I was black and streaked with sweat;
And poked it out then, with charred meat still clustering
Thick around the bones. And buried it so
As I should have done in the first place, for
The earth is slow, but deep, and good for hiding;

I would have used it if I had understood
How nine lives can vanish in one flash of a dog's jaws,
A car or a copperhead, and yet how one small
Death, however reckoned, is hard to dispose of.

DOG DREAMING

The paws twitch in a place of chasing
Where the whimper of this seeming-gentle creature
Rings out terrible, chasing tigers. The fields
Are licking like torches, full of running,
Laced odours, bones stalking, tushed leaps.
So little that is tamed, yet so much
That you would find deeply familiar there.
You are there often, your very eyes,
The unfathomable knowledge behind your face,
The mystery of your will, appraising
Such carnage and triumph; standing there
Strange even to yourself, and loved, and only
A sleeping beast knows who you are.

BACKWATER POND: THE CANOEISTS

Not for the fishermen's sake
Do they drop their voices as they glide in from the lake,
And take to moving stealthily on that still water,
Not to disturb its stillness, hour on hour.
So that when at last a turtle, scuttling
Surprised from a stump, dives with a sudden splashing,
It startles them like a door slamming;
And then there is a faint breeze and echo of laughter
Dying as quickly, and they float still as before
Like shadows sliding over a mirror
Or clouds across some forgotten sky,
All afternoon, they cannot say why.

RIVER SOUND REMEMBERED

That day the huge water drowned all voices until
It seemed a kind of silence unbroken
By anything: a time unto itself and still;

So that when I turned away from its roaring, down
The path over the gully, and there were
Dogs barking as always at the edge of town,

Car horns and the cries of children coming
As though for the first time through the fading light
Of the winter dusk, my ears still sang

Like shells with the swingeing current, and
Its flood echoing in me held for long
About me the same silence, by whose sound

I could hear only the quiet under the day
With the land noises floating there far-off and still;
So that even in my mind now turning away

From having listened absently but for so long
It will be the seethe and drag of the river
That I will hear longer than any mortal song.

AFTER THE FLOOD

The morning it was over, I walked
To the Jersey side, where there is a park,
And where even in summer the river
Is at least two feet higher than it is on our side,
Because of the way it bends. It had not been
A bad rise, such as many remember.
A line of flotsam, full of
Exotic-looking dark foliage stretched
Cross-wise through the park, just meeting
The river wall at the end corner. Things
I felt I must surely remember, they looked so
Familiar, had fished up there with sudden
Histories to them that would never get told.
I remembered how I had climbed the dike
Two days before, when the lower bridge
Was in danger. Coming in sight of the river then
The amazing thing was how much
More quiet the swollen water seemed
Than I had expected, how slowly
It seemed to move, like some beast sneaking.
Now it seemed noisy again, but I could hear
Other sounds coming over it. A sea-gull creaking,
Not tempted by the miserable leavings.
Almost disappointed myself, I made myself
Think of how much we had been spared,
How much that was cherished had, other times,
Been swept down the river. I noticed
Near the bottom of the park, just below
The high-water line, an old coat hanging
Snagged on a tree-branch, and caught myself wondering
What sort of drunken creature had passed there.

IN THE HEART OF EUROPE

Farmers hereabouts, for generations now
Have owned their own places; their names
Covered the country before the families
Of the former kings were heard of, and having
Survived masters and serfdom, describe still the same spot.
They partake of their land's very features: it is
Theirs as it can be no others'. What keeps and has
Kept them? Can you call it love
That is a habit so ancient that a man's span
Is brief in its practice; whose beginnings
Are no more remembered than the hills' genesis? A thing
Inexplicable, but so casual, and for which
They have no names but their own? Why, even,
They build their houses that way, they could never tell you.
It is as though, in a thing so established
They knew themselves tenants, merely, till the country
Turns from them to their children. You feel they would never
Say the place belonged to them: a reticence
Like love's delicacy or its quiet assurance.

A SPARROW SHELTERING UNDER A COLUMN
OF THE BRITISH MUSEUM

Conceived first by whom? By the Greeks perfected,
By the Romans, the Rennaissance and the Victorians copied,

Almost from the first more massive than our uses
And so indicating something more, the stone rises

Into the clear sunlight rare for a London January.
Why about columns does it seem always windy?

Still, he restores this one to bare use, convenient
For huddling between its base and pediment

Where though the wind still ruffles him it is somewhat broken.
Porches are places of passage; and again

To us they indicate something beyond; to him
Its shape and position in the wind are the column.

And whereas to him the feet of children and scholars
Who pass all day through the merely useful doors

To enquire of the rich uncertainty of their farthing
Are not shaped like danger unless too near, may even bring

Crumbs to offer to a necessity
Which they both conciliate so differently,

(He, alive not to limits but presences,
They hungering less for shapes than significances)

Skelton's bird or Catullus's, or even
That pair whose fall figured our need of heaven

Would mean nothing to him, for he would never
Recognize them as now they are

Beyond doors there, where the wind is unknown,
But knows simply that this stone

Shelters, rising into the native air,
And that, though perhaps cold, he is at home there.

LEARNING A DEAD LANGUAGE

There is nothing for you to say. You must
Learn first to listen. Because it is dead
It will not come to you of itself, nor would you
Of yourself master it. You must therefore
Learn to be still when it is imparted,
And, though you may not yet understand, to remember.

What you remember is saved. To understand
The least thing fully you would have to perceive
The whole grammar in all its accidence
And all its system, in the perfect singleness
Of intention it has because it is dead.
You can learn only a part at a time.

What you are given to remember
Has been saved before you from death's dullness by
Remembering. The unique intention
Of a language whose speech has died is order
Incomplete only where someone has forgotten.
You will find that that order helps you to remember.

What you come to remember becomes yourself.
Learning will be to cultivate the awareness
Of that governing order, now pure of the passions
It composed; till, seeking it in itself,
You may find at last the passion that composed it,
Hear it both in its speech and in yourself.

What you remember saves you. To remember
Is not to rehearse, but to hear what never
Has fallen silent. So your learning is,
From the dead, order, and what sense of yourself
Is memorable, what passion may be heard
When there is nothing for you to say.

THREE FACES

In half profile, one behind the other,
As in a Greek frieze the edges of horses
One behind the other; between them
A family resemblance, no more:
Not the multiplied identity
Which in the drunkard's vision spreads and shifts,
Nor the unity of the Trinity.

All three, looming long as the heads of horses,
Are shaped as tears falling upwards in a wind
Whose darkness fashions them, defining
In each the pallid half-light, vast eyes,
Distorting them singly and together to those
Irregularities which are their features.
Chins in their hands, elbows on solid darkness.

So their differences are of darkness,
Whose reflection three times varied in
Their eyes, shows not itself but them
Changing on one hand and on the other
Through gradations which must be infinite;
And yet their shape it is, and common nature,
And to their partial spectrum the white light.

HER WISDOM

So is she with love's tenderness
Made tender—and touched tenderness is pain;
Pain in fit subject distorts or burns into wisdom—

That she both by usual things and presences
Too delicate for usual ears and eyes
At all hands is touched and made wise,

Being instructed by stones of their rough childhoods,
In the migratory tides of birds seeing the cold
Hand of the moon and the shape of their shore;

She suffers too the noise of night's shadow flexing
Invisible in the unrustling air of noon,
With a sound between parchment stretched and a bat's squeak;

Is aware at all hours of the scream and sigh
Of shadows, of each moment: things forever violated,
Forever virgin; hears sleep falling wherever it falls.

Such understanding, uncommunicable
To other senses, and seeming so simple,
Is more a mystery than things not known at all;

For pain is common, but learned of not often,
Taught never; and who, could she speak it,
Would have ears to hear? She would not if she could,

Because of her tenderness. But should
Love's wisdom so wound her that she die
Would the knowledge then to which she succumbed

Most resemble the fear which we hear in the leaves' falling,
Hope as it falters in our failing questions,
Or joy as it overtakes us even in pain?

THE SAPPHIRE

After a dream in which your love's fullness
Was heaven and earth, I stood on nothing in darkness,
Neither finding nor falling, without hope nor dread,
Not knowing pleasure nor discontented.
In time, like the first beam arriving from
The first star, a ray from a seed of light came,
Whose source, coming nearer, (I could not say whether
It rose or descended, for there was no higher nor lower)
To a trumpet's thin sweet highest note
Which grew to the pitch of pain, showed how its white
Light proceeded all from a blue crystal stone
Large as a child's skull, shaped so, lucent as when
Daylight strikes sideways through a cat's eyes;
Blue not blinding, its light did not shine but was;
And came, as the trumpet pierced through into silence,
To hover so close before my hands
That I might have held it, but that one does not handle
What one accepts as a miracle.
A great sapphire it was whose light and cradle
Held all things: there were the delights of skies, though
Its cloudless blue was different; of sea and meadow,
But their shapes not seen. The stone unheld was mine,
But yours the sense by which, without further sign
I recognized its visionary presence
By its clarity, its changeless patience,
And the unuttered joy that it was,
As the world's love before the world was.

THORN LEAVES IN MARCH

Walking out in the late March midnight
With the old blind bitch on her bedtime errand
Of ease stumbling beside me, I saw

At the hill's edge, by the blue flooding
Of the arc-lamps, and the moon's suffused presence
The first leaves budding pale on the thorn trees,

Uncurling with that crass light coming through them,
Like the translucent wings of insects
Dilating in the dampness of birth;

And their green seemed already more ghostly
Than the hour drowned beneath bells, and the city sleeping,
Or even than the month with its round moon sinking.

As a white lamb the month's entrance had been:
The day warm, and at night unexpectedly
An hour of soft snow falling silently,

Soon ceasing, leaving transfigured all traceries,
These shrubs and trees, in white and white shadows; silk screens
Where were fences. And all restored again in an hour.

And as a lamb, I could see now, it would go,
Breathless, into its own ghostliness,
Taking with it more than its tepid moon.

And here there would be no lion at all that is
The beast of gold, and sought as an answer,
Whose pure sign in no solution is,

But between its two lambs the month would have run
As its varying moon, all silver,
That is the colour of questions.

Oh there as it went was such a silence
Before the water of April should be heard singing
Strangely as ever under the knowing ground

As fostered in me the motion of asking
In hope of no answer that fated leaves,
Sleep, or the sinking moon might proffer,

And in no words, but as it seemed in love only
For all breath, whose departing nature is
The spirit of question, whatever least I knew,

Whatever most I wondered. In which devotion
I stayed until the bell struck and the silver
Ebbed before April, and might have stood unseizing

Among answers less ghostly than the first leaves
On the thorn trees, since to seize had been
Neither to love nor to possess;

While the old bitch nosed and winded, conjuring
A congenial spot, and the constellations
Sank nearer already, listing toward summer.

LOW FIELDS AND LIGHT

I think it is in Virginia, that place
That lies across the eye of my mind now
Like a grey blade set to the moon's roundness,
Like a plain of glass touching all there is.

The flat fields run out to the sea there.
There is no sand, no line. It is autumn.
The bare fields, dark between fences, run
Out to the idle gleam of the flat water.

And the fences go on out, sinking slowly,
With a cow-bird half-way, on a stunted post, watching
How the light slides through them easy as weeds
Or wind, slides over them away out near the sky

Because even a bird can remember
The fields that were there before the slow
Spread and wash of the edging light crawled
There and covered them, a little more each year.

My father never plowed there, nor my mother
Waited, and never knowingly I stood there
Hearing the seepage slow as growth, nor knew
When the taste of salt took over the ground.

But you would think the fields were something
To me, so long I stare out, looking
For their shapes or shadows through the matted gleam, seeing
Neither what is nor what was, but the flat light rising.

BIRDS WAKING

I went out at daybreak and stood on Primrose Hill.
It was April: a white haze over the hills of Surrey
Over the green haze of the hills above the dark green
Of the park trees, and over it all the light came up clear,
The sky like deep porcelain paling and paling,
With everywhere under it the faces of the buildings
Where the city slept, gleaming white and quiet,
St Paul's and the water tower taking the gentle gold.
And from the hill chestnuts and the park trees
There was such a clamour rose as the birds woke,
Such uncontainable tempest of whirled
Singing flung upward and upward into the new light,
Increasing still as the birds themselves rose
From the black trees and whirled in a rising cloud,
Flakes and water-spouts and hurled seas and continents of them
Rising, dissolving, streamering out, always
Louder and louder singing, shrieking, laughing.
Sometimes one would break from the cloud but from the song
     never,
And would beat past my ear dinning his deafening note.
I thought I had never known the wind
Of joy to be so shrill, so unanswerable,
With such clouds of winged song at its disposal, and I thought
Oh Voice that my demand is the newest name for,
There are many ways we may end, and one we must,
Whether burning, or the utter cold descending in darkness,
Explosion of our own devising, collision of planets, all
Violent, however silent they at last may seem;
Oh let it be by this violence, then, let it be now,
Now when in their sleep, unhearing, unknowing,

Most faces must be closest to innocence,
When the light moves unhesitating to fill the sky with clearness
And no dissent could be heard above the din of its welcome,
Let the great globe well up and dissolve like its last birds,
With the bursting roar and uprush of song!

PART THREE

EVENING WITH LEE SHORE AND CLIFFS

Sea-shimmer, faint haze, and far out a bird
Dipping for flies or fish. Then, when over
That wide silk suddenly the shadow
Spread skating, who turned with a shiver
High in the rocks? And knew, then only, the waves'
Layering patience: how they would follow after,
After, dogged as sleep, to his inland
Dreams, oh beyond the one lamb that cried
In the olives, past the pines' derision. And heard
Behind him not the sea's gaiety but its laughter.

THE FISHERMEN

When you think how big their feet are in black rubber
And it slippery underfoot always, it is clever
How they thread and manage among the sprawled nets, lines,
Hooks, spidery cages with small entrances.
But they are used to it. We do not know their names.
They know our needs, and live by them, lending them wiles
And beguilements we could never have fashioned for them;
They carry the ends of our hungers out to drop them
To wait swaying in a dark place we could never have chosen.
By motions we have never learned they feed us.
We lay wreaths on the sea when it has drowned them.

TWO PAINTINGS BY ALFRED WALLIS

i

Voyage to Labrador

Tonight when the sea runs like a sore,
Swollen as hay and with the same sound,
Where under the hat-dark the iron
Ship slides seething, hull crammed
With clamours the fluttering hues of a fever,
Clang-battened in, the stunned bells done
From the rung-down quartans, and only
The dotty lights still trimmed
Abroad like teeth, there dog-hunched will the high
Street of hugging bergs have come
To lean huge and hidden as women,
Untouched as smoke and, at our passing, pleased
Down to the private sinks of their cold.
Then we will be white, all white, as cloths sheening,
Stiff as teeth, white as the sticks
And eyes of the blind. But morning, mindless
And uncaring as Jesus, will find nothing
In that same place but an empty sea
Colourless, see, as a glass of water.

ii

Schooner Under the Moon

Waits where we would almost be. Part
Pink as a tongue; floats high on the olive
Rumpled night-flood, foresails and clouds hiding
Such threat and beauty as we may never see.

189

SENILITY CAY

Like a nail-paring cast from the moon's leprosy
The beach sheens white to the moon's tooth;
All the birds are dying along the sand, you would say
A camp croaking feeble with a fever;
Grey grass twitching like cheeks, and the scurf
Crawling dry on the palsied sea.
Not a sail there. Not a face in sight. But here
Thin as a fish-bone, left open so it stares
Is the gaunt gap where what was a man will be.

FOG

You see, shore-hugging is neither surety
Nor earns salt pride braving the long sea-sweeps.
This came up in the dark while some of us
Bore on in our sleep. Was there
In the dog-watch already, hiding the dog-star.
We woke into it, rising from dreams
Of sea-farms slanting on cliffs in clear light
And white houses winking there—sweet landmarks
But no help to us at the helm. Hours now
We have been drifting. It would be near noon.
Feeling the tides fight under our feet
Like a crawling of carpets. Turning our heads
To pick up the cape-bell, the hoots of the shoal-horn
That seem to come from all over. Distrusting
Every direction that is simple, to shoreward. This
Landfall is not vouchsafed us for
We have abused landfalls, loving them wrong
And too timorously. What coastline
Will not cloud over if looked at long enough?
Not through the rings running with us of enough
Horizons, not wide enough risking,
Not hard enough have we wrought our homing.
Drifting itself now is danger. Where are we?
Well, the needle swings still to north, and we know
Even in this blindness which way deep water lies.
Ships were not shaped for haven but if we were
There will be time for it yet. Let us turn head,
Out oars, and pull for the open. Make we

For mid-sea, where the winds are and stars too.
There will be wrung weathers, sea-shakings, calms,
Weariness, the giant water that rolls over our fathers,
And hungers hard to endure. But whether we float long
Or founder soon, we cannot be saved here.

THE SHIPWRECK

The tale is different if even a single breath
Escapes to tell it. The return itself
Says survival is possible. And words made to carry
In quiet the burden, the isolation
Of dust, and that fail even so,
Though they shudder still, must shrink the great head
Of elemental violence, the vast eyes
Called blind looking into the ends of darkness,
The mouth deafening understanding with its one
All-wise syllable, into a shrivelled
History that the dry-shod may hold
In the palms of their hands. They had her
Under jib and reefed mizzen, and in the dark
Were fairly sure where they were, and with sea-room,
And it seemed to be slacking a little, until
Just before three they struck. Heard
It come home, hollow in the hearts of them,
And only then heard the bell ringing, telling them
It had been ringing there always telling them
That there it would strike home, hollow, in
The hearts of them. Only then heard it
Over the sunlight, the dozing creak
Of the moorings, the bleaching quay, the heat,
The coiled ropes on the quay the day they would sail
And the day before, and across the water blue
As a sky through the heat beyond
The coils, the coils, with their shadows coiled
Inside them. And it sprang upon them dark,
Bitter, and heavy with sound. They began to go
To pieces at once under the waves' hammer.

Sick at heart since that first stroke, they moved
Nevertheless as they had learned always to move
When it should come, not weighing hope against
The weight of the water, yet knowing that no breath
Would escape to betray what they underwent then.
Dazed too, incredulous, that it had come,
That they could recognize it. It was too familiar,
And they in the press of it, therefore, as though
In a drifting dream. But it bore in upon them
Bursting slowly inside them where they had
Coiled it down, coiled it down: this sea, it was
Blind, yes, as they had said, and treacherous—
They had used their own traits to character it—but without
Accident in its wildness, in its rage,
Utterly and from the beginning without
Error. And to some it seemed that the waves
Grew gentle, spared them, while they died of that knowledge.

THE EYES OF THE DROWNED WATCH KEELS
GOING OVER

Where the light has no horizons we lie.
It dims into depth not distance. It sways
Like hair, then we shift and turn over slightly.
As once on the long swing under the trees
In the drowse of summer we slid to and fro
Slowly in the soft wash of the air, looking
Upwards through the leaves that turned over and back
Like hands, through the birds, the fathomless light,
Upwards. They go over us swinging
Jaggedly, labouring between our eyes
And the light. Churning their wrought courses
Between the sailing birds and the awed eyes
Of the fish, with the grace of neither, nor with
The stars' serenity that they follow.
Yet the light shakes around them as they go.
Why? And why should we, rocking on shoal-pillow,
With our eyes cling to them, and their wakes follow,
Who follow nothing? If we could remember
The stars in their clarity, we might understand now
Why we pursued stars, to what end our eyes
Fastened upon stars, how it was that we traced
In their remote courses not their own fates but ours.

MARINERS' CAROL

So still the night swinging,
Wind of our faring,
Only the bows' seethe to lap us,
Stays and wake whispering,
The thin bell striking,
And our hearts in their blindness.
O star, shine before us!

The serpent's deep sliding,
Wind of our faring,
Is everywhere around us,
Heaves under us, gliding;
We know its toothed curling
The whole world encircles.
O star, shine before us!

Crushed in its drag and keeping,
Wind of our faring,
The darkened dead have no peace,
World-without-end shifting;
All, all are there, and no resting.
It exults above their faces.
O star, shine before us!

The horizon's perfect ring,
Wind of our faring,
None enters nor ever has.
And we, like a cradle, rocking:
For the first glimpse of our homing
We roll and are restless.
O star, shine before us!

196

Till, heaven and earth joining,
Wind of our faring,
It is born to us
Like the first line of dawn breaking;
For that word and sight yearning
We keep the long watches.
O star, shine before us!

The Drunk in the Furnace

(1960)

FOR MY MOTHER AND FATHER

ODYSSEUS

for George Kirstein

Always the setting forth was the same,
Same sea, same dangers waiting for him
As though he had got nowhere but older.
Behind him on the receding shore
The identical reproaches, and somewhere
Out before him, the unravelling patience
He was wedded to. There were the islands
Each with its woman and twining welcome
To be navigated, and one to call "home."
The knowledge of all that he betrayed
Grew till it was the same whether he stayed
Or went. Therefore he went. And what wonder
If sometimes he could not remember
Which was the one who wished on his departure
Perils that he could never sail through,
And which, improbable, remote, and true,
Was the one he kept sailing home to?

THE ICEBERG

It is not its air but our own awe
That freezes us. Hardest of all to believe
That so fearsome a destroyer can be
Dead, with those lights moving in it,
With the sea all around it charged
With its influence. It seems that only now
We realize the depth of the waters, the
Abyss over which we float among such
Clouds. And still not understanding
The coldness of most elegance, even
With so vast and heartless a splendor
Before us, stare, caught in the magnetism
Of great silence, thinking: this is the terror
That cannot be charted, this is only
A little of it. And recall how many
Mariners, watching the sun set, have seen
These peaks on the horizon and made sail
Through the darkness for islands that no map
Had promised, floating blessèd in
The west. These must dissolve
Before they can again grow apple trees.

FOG-HORN

Surely that moan is not the thing
That men thought they were making, when they
Put it there, for their own necessities.
That throat does not call to anything human
But to something men had forgotten,
That stirs under fog. Who wounded that beast
Incurably, or from whose pasture
Was it lost, full grown, and time closed round it
With no way back? Who tethered its tongue
So that its voice could never come
To speak out in the light of clear day,
But only when the shifting blindness
Descends and is acknowledged among us,
As though from under a floor it is heard,
Or as though from behind a wall, always
Nearer than we had remembered? If it
Was we that gave tongue to this cry
What does it bespeak in us, repeating
And repeating, insisting on something
That we never meant? We only put it there
To give warning of something we dare not
Ignore, lest we should come upon it
Too suddenly, recognize it too late,
As our cries were swallowed up and all hands lost.

DECEPTION ISLAND

for Arthur Mizener

You can go farther. The south itself
Goes much farther, hundreds of miles, first
By sea, then over the white continent,
Mountainous, unmapped, all the way to the pole.

But sometimes imagination
Is content to rest here, at harbor
In the smooth bay in the dead mountain,
Like a vessel at anchor in its own reflection.

The glassy roadstead sleeps in a wide ring
Of ice and igneous shingle, whose gradual
Slopes rise, under streaks of white and black all
The swept shapes of wind, to the volcano's ridges.

It is like being suspended in the open
Vast wreck of a stony skull dead for ages.
You cannot believe the crater was ever
Fiery, before it filled with silence, and sea.

It is not a place you would fancy
You would like to go to. The slopes are barren
Of all the vegetation of desire.
But a place to imagine lying at anchor,

Watching the sea outside the broken
Temple of the cold fire-head, and wondering

Less at the wastes of silence and distance
Than at what all that lonely fire was for.

SEA WIFE

There must be so many souls washing
Up and down out there just out of sight,
You would think the sea would be full; one day
It will surely be full and no more sea.
We will not live to see it. You can see
That the eyes of fish, used to staring at souls,
Can never believe us: standing up and breathing air.
So much the sea changes things. Husbands
Maybe you never know, but sons, fathers,
Above all brothers—they are fished from us
And gone in the holds of boats, and only
Strangers come in to us from the sea, even
If sometimes they be the same strangers.
Or else their names, sounding like strangers, on
The church wall. Us too it changes; just
With hating it our eyes take on its distance
And our hair its blowing whiteness. But we
Are the same, here with God and the bells. And the boats,
Maybe they are the same when we see them.
But we were never close to them, they were always
Untouchable as though in bottles. Do not learn it
From us; the bells are old and impartial
And upright and will tell you: beyond
The last channel nun and the cape horn
God is not righteous, doom calls like women,
The fish wait for friends. God is our rock here
In His goodness. The bells tell where He is.
They tell of His righteousness, and they moan seaward
Mourning for the souls, the souls, that are lost there.

THE FROZEN SEA

We walked on it, in the very flesh
No different only colder, as was
The sea itself. It was simple as that.
Only, the wind would not have it, would not
Have it: the whiteness at last
Bearing us up where we would go. Screamed
With lungs we would never have guessed at,
Shrieked round us, whipping up the cold crust,
Lashing the rigid swell into dust. It would
Find the waves for us, or freeze out
The mortal flaw in us: then we might stay.
And it was right: it was not any light
From heaven that hurt our eyes, but
The whiteness that we could not bear. It
Turned bloody in our carnal eyes. Virtues
That had borne us thus far turned on us, peopling
The lashed plains of our minds with hollow voices
Out of the snouted masks of beasts. Their
Guts would feed on God, they said. But danger
Had given shape, stiffening shape, to our
Pride, and that sustained us in silence
As we went over that screaming silence.
Yet how small we were around whom the howling
World turned. We could not see half a mile.
And only a soulless needle to tell us where
In the round world we were. We had come so far
To whiteness, and it was cruel in our eyes,
To the pure south, and whichever way we turned
Was north, the sides of the north, everywhere.

SAILOR ASHORE

What unsteady ways the solid earth has
After all. The lamps are dead on their feet
Blinking and swaying above the wet cobbles;
The darkness yaws out and back, sprawling
And slithering on the walls; the sleeping houses
Reel and almost fall but never wake;
And the echo of feet goes round and round
Like a buffeted gull, and can find no place
To alight. Somebody said it would be
Like this: the sea is everywhere.
But worst here where it is secret and pretends
To keep its mountains in one place. If you
Put your foot down the spot moves: the waters are
Under the earth. Nowhere to run from them.
It is their tides you feel heaving under you,
Sucking you down, when you close your eyes with women.
They wink in bottles, and you are washed off
And under. Gull shriek, boozy guffaw, woman
Laughing—turn your back on each in turn
And you hear the waters' laughter. Which is
What they gave you a back for. Better to stay
In one place, and sleep like the lamps, standing;
Then get back to the bare-faced original
Bitch-sea. Which is what they gave you legs for.

THE *PORTLAND* GOING OUT

Early that afternoon, as we keep
Remembering, the water of the harbor
Was so smooth you wanted to walk on it,
It looked that trustworthy: glassy and black
Like one of those pools they have in the lobbies
Of grand hotels. And, thinking back, we say
That the same bells we had heard telling
Their shoals and hours since we were children,
Sounded different, as though they were
Moving about the business of strangers. By
Five it was kicking up quite a bit,
And the greasiest evening you ever saw,
We had just come in, and were making fast,
A few minutes to seven, when she went
Down the harbor behind us, going out,
Passing so close over our stern that we
Caught the red glow of her port light for
A moment on our faces. Only
When she was gone did we notice
That it was starting to snow. No, we were
Not the last, nor even nearly the last
To see her. A schooner that lived through it
Glimpsed her, at the height of the storm,
In a clear patch, apparently riding it;
That must have been no more than minutes
Before she went down. We had known storms
Before, almost as brutal, and wrecks before
Almost as unexplained, almost
As disastrous. Yet we keep asking
How it happened, how, and why Blanchard sailed,

Miscalculating the storm's course. But what
We cannot even find questions for
Is how near we were: brushed by the same snow,
Lifted by her wake as she passed. We could
Have spoken, we swear, with anyone on her deck,
And not had to raise our voices, if we
Had known anything to say. And now
In no time at all, she has put
All of disaster between us: a gulf
Beyond reckoning. It begins where we are.

SEA MONSTER

We were not even out of sight of land
That afternoon when we saw it. A good day
With the sea making but still light. Not
One of us would have hesitated
As to where we were, or mistaken the brown
Cliffs or the town on top. Just after
The noon watch, it was, that it slid
Into our sight: a darkness under
The surface, between us and the land, twisting
Like a snake swimming or a line of birds
In the air. Then breached, big as a church,
Right there beside us. None of us will
Agree what it was we saw then, but
None of us showed the least surprise, and truly
I felt none. I would say its eyes
Were like the sea when the thick snow falls
Onto it with a whisper and slides heaving
On the gray water. And looked at us
For a long time, as though it knew us, but
Did not harm us that time, sinking at last,
The waters closing like a rush of breath. Then
We were all ashamed at what we had seen,
Said it was only a sea-trick or
A dream we had all had together. As it
May have been, for since then we have forgotten
How it was that, on sea or land, once
We proved to ourselves that we were awake.

CAPE DREAD

For those who come after, that is how we named it;
You may find that some other suits it better. Only
We pray you, for no saint christen it. The toll of us
That it took, we do not yet know the unhallowed
End of it, any more than we can assess
Our own ends beforehand. All summer
We had coursed a strange ocean, the winds driving
From quarters that seemed unnatural, and the set
Of the currents sorted not with our learning.
But in autumn sometimes all waters seem familiar,
With leaves, quite far out, littering the ground swell
On smooth days when the wind is light. And in
The haze then you can believe you are anywhere:
Standing off a home shore, and can even smell
The sweet dankness of smoke from known hearths. So we
Bore on, feeling courage more fresh in us
Than on the day of our sailing, musing
How far we might fetch before winter. Then
Through the mist we raised it, the abrupt cape
Looming dark and too near to leeward;
And recognized, like a home-thought too, in that landfall
The other side of autumn: that the year
Would bear us no farther, that we would not
Get beyond this. Perhaps it was named
At that moment in our minds, when we sighted
The shape of what we knew we would not pass.
You cannot mistake it: the dun headland
Like a dreaming Dutchman, dough-faced, staring
Seaward to the side we did not penetrate.
You almost think he will turn as you

Grope your way in with the lead-line. Hope suddenly
Was as far behind us as home, and maybe
That made us clumsy, dull of heart going in.
But the waters are treacherous off that point,
With a fierce knot of currents twisting, even
At slack-tide, snatching you from your seaway,
Sucking over a jagged shelving, and there is
Rough shoal beyond that. Three ships we lost
And many of their men there, and only we
Because we were driven far to port, almost
To the drag at the cliff's foot, and made in
Through the very spray, found the channel. There is
Nine fathoms all the way in there, to the broad pool
Of quiet water behind the tide-race;
You can anchor in five fathoms at
The lowest tide, with good holding, and sheltered.
You will use the harbor; in other years you will
Set out from there, in the spring, and think
Of that headland as home, calling it Cape
Delight, or Dutchman's Point. But what we found
You will find for yourselves, somewhere, for
Yourselves. We have not gone there again,
Nor ventured ever so far again. In
The south corner of the cove there is
An inlet flowing with sweet water,
And there are fruits in abundance, small
But delectable, at least at that season.

BELL BUOY

So we set signs over the world to say
To ourselves, returning, that we know the place,
Marking the sea too with shaped tokens
Of our usage, which even while they serve us
Make one with the unmeasured mist, sea-slap,
Green rock awash with the gray heave just
Out of sight, wet air saturated with sounds
But no breath—and in no time they are seen
To be in league with the world's remoteness
Whose features we grope for through fog and can never
Seize to our satisfaction. First the sound
Comes, and again, from the caged bell lost in the gray
Out ahead. Then into the glasses,
And gone, and again sighted, staying:
A black shape like nothing, rounded, rocking like
A chair, with a gull on top. Clearer
The dreaming bronze clangs over the lifting
Swell, through the fog-drift, clangs, not
On the sea-stroke but on the fifth second clangs,
Recalling something, out of some absence
We cannot fathom, with itself communing.
Was it we who made this, or the sea's necessity?
You can hear the wash on its rolling plates
Over your own wake, as you come near
And confirm: black can, odd number crusted
Already with gull crap over the new paint,
Green beard and rust speckling its undersides
As you see when it rolls. Nothing you can
Say as you pass, though there are only you two
And you come so close and seem to share

So much. And it will twist and stare after you
Through the closing fog, clanging. It is
A dead thing but we have agreed upon it: kept
To port, entering, starboard departing, as
May your fortune be, it can assure you
Of where you are, though it knows nothing
Of where you are going or may have been.

THE BONES

It takes a long time to hear what the sands
Seem to be saying, with the wind nudging them,
And then you cannot put it in words nor tell
Why these things should have a voice. All kinds
Of objects come in over the tide-wastes
In the course of a year, with a throaty
Rattle: weeds, driftwood, the bodies of birds
And of fish, shells. For years I had hardly
Considered shells as being bones, maybe
Because of the sound they could still make, though
I knew a man once who could raise a kind
Of wailing tune out of a flute he had,
Made from a fibula: it was much the same
Register as the shells'; the tune did not
Go on when his breath stopped, though you thought it would.
Then that morning, coming on the wreck,
I saw the kinship. No recent disaster
But an old ghost from under a green buoy,
Brought in by the last storm, or one from which
The big wind had peeled back the sand grave
To show what was still left: the bleached, chewed-off
Timbers like the ribs of a man or the jaw-bone
Of some extinct beast. Far down the sands its
Broken cage leaned out, casting no shadow
In the veiled light. There was a man sitting beside it
Eating out of a paper, littering the beach
With the bones of a few more fish, while the hulk
Cupped its empty hand high over him. Only he
And I had come to those sands knowing
That they were there. The rest was bones, whatever

Tunes they made. The bones of things; and of men too
And of man's endeavors whose ribs he had set
Between himself and the shapeless tides. Then
I saw how the sand was shifting like water,
That once could walk. Shells were to shut out the sea,
The bones of birds were built for floating
On air and water, and those of fish were devised
For their feeding depths, while a man's bones were framed
For what? For knowing the sands are here,
And coming to hear them a long time; for giving
Shapes to the sprawled sea, weight to its winds,
And wrecks to plead for its sands. These things are not
Limitless: we know there is somewhere
An end to them, though every way you look
They extend farther than a man can see.

THE HIGHWAY

It seems too enormous just for a man to be
Walking on. As if it and the empty day
Were all there is. And a little dog
Trotting in time with the heat waves, off
Near the horizon, seeming never to get
Any farther. The sun and everything
Are stuck in the same places, and the ditch
Is the same all the time, full of every kind
Of bone, while the empty air keeps humming
That sound it has memorized of things going
Past. And the signs with huge heads and starved
Bodies, doing dances in the heat,
And the others big as houses, all promise
But with nothing inside and only one wall,
Tell of other places where you can eat,
Drink, get a bath, lie on a bed
Listening to music, and be safe. If you
Look around you see it is just the same
The other way, going back; and farther
Now to where you came from, probably,
Than to places you can reach by going on.

FABLE

However the man had got himself there,
There he clung, kicking in mid-air,
Hanging from the top branch of a high tree
With his grip weakening gradually.
A passer-by who noticed him
Moved a safe distance from under the limb,
And then stood with his arms akimbo, calling,
"Let go, or you'll be killed; the tree is falling."
The man up on the branch, blindly clinging,
With his face toward heaven, and his knees heaving,
Heard this, through his depending to and fro,
And with his last ounce of good faith, let go.
No creature could have survived that fall,
And the stranger was not surprised at all
To find him dead, but told his body, "You
Only let go because you wanted to;
All you lacked was a good reason.
I let you hope you might save your skin
By taking the most comfortable way."
Then added, smiling, as he walked away,
"Besides, you'd have fallen anyway."

LUTHER

That old slider, the Prince of Falsehood,
I could recognize him in my cradle.
Though masked as the preacher, he took the pulpit,
Though he appeared as a swine, as a burning
Wisp of straw, or would be dandled in
The shape of an infant, always I could
Name him out. And yet there he stood
Mocking me with a scholar's prim tone,
Insisting that I could not say
What he was, with any authority;
Smiling to remind me that Holy
Church alone could pronounce him other
Than my own image, gnarled in my mind's mirror,
But that Holy Church might, for pay,
Countenance even that aspect of me
And indulge it with kindlier names
Than Evil. Then I flung the inkwell.
And every man may know the devil
From this day forth, who can tell
Black from white, for the devil
Is black. He is black. I have made him so.

BUCOLIC

Having enough plowshares,
The best will in the world, and fat pastures,
They beat the rest of their swords into shears.

The rewards of peace
They reap! With each haired, maned, shag beast,
As each tamed field, fattened for its fleece.

If, as of old,
But with stuffed bellies, the shorn wolves seek the fold,
It is only in winter, from the cold:

Whole days, when the snow is deep,
They lie, pink and harmless, among the sheep,
Nodding, whether in agreement or sleep.

UNDER THE OLD ONE

Helpless improver,
Grown numerous and clever
Rather than wise or loving,
Nothing is newer than ever
Under the sun:

Still specious, wanton, venal,
Your noises as dull
And smiles self-flattering
As was usual
Under any heaven.

How often, before this,
You went on knees
To moons of your own making,
Abject, with no peace
Under the old one.

NO ONE

Who would it surprise
If (after the flash, hush, rush,
Thump and crumpling) when the wind of prophecy
Lifts its pitch, and over the drifting ash
At last the trump splits the sky,
No One should arise

(No one just as before:
No limbs, eyes, presence;
Mindless and incorruptible) to inherit
Without question the opening heavens,
To be alone, to be complete,
And so forever?

Who had kept our secrets,
Whose wisdom we had heeded,
Who had stood near us (we proved it) again
And again in the dark, to whom we had prayed
Naturally and most often,
Who had escaped our malice—

No more than equitable
By No One to be succeeded,
Who had known our merits, had believed
Our lies, before ourselves whom we had considered
And (after ourselves) had loved
Constantly and well.

IN A CLOUD OF HANDS

Shadows shaped like rabbits and the mottlings
Of cats shake loose into a frenzy
Of gesticulation, with a sound
Of washing, and as you were aware
The whole night is alive with hands,

Is aflame with palms and offerings
And racked with a soft yammer for alms
Disclosing always the same craving
Through the three seasons of leaves
And in mid-winter when the trees
Are hung with empty gloves all over:
The coin called out for is ourselves.

As you knew, you knew, born into hands,
To be handed away, in time.

Meantime these soft gordians
The fists of infants, these hands,
Padded crabs raining their prints
As on charts the contours of islands,
Vulnerable as eyes, these fans
Without feathers, knuckled sticks over
Breasts flowing like shawls or sea water,
That can learn flights exact as swallows,
Make music, pain, prayer, these
Rags dangling like moss from ancient wrists,

Loose, are sometimes generous,
Closed, can hold fast for a time;

Uncurled, as in supplication, empty
As crystals and shallow as dry lagoons
Scrawled over by water-bugs, what have they
To offer but love in ignorance,
Uncertain even of its own questions,
As of the maps on its hands, whether
They lead anywhere at all.

IN STONY COUNTRY

Somewhere else than these bare uplands dig wells,
Expect flowers, listen to sheep bells.
Wind; no welcome; and nowhere else
Pillows like these stones for dreaming of angels.

CATULLUS XI

Furius and Aurelius, bound to Catullus
Though he penetrate to the ends of the Indies
Where the eastern ocean crashing in echoes
    Pours up the shore,

Or into Hyrcania, soft Arabia,
Among Tartars or the archers of Parthia,
Or where the Nile current, seven times the same,
    Colors the waters,

Or through the beetling Alps, by steep passes, should come
To look on the monuments of great Caesar,
Gaul, the Rhine, and at the world's bitter end
    The gruesome Britons,

Friends, both prepared to share with me all these
Or what else the will of heaven may send,
To my mistress take these few sentiments,
    Put none too nicely:

Let her spread for her lechers and get her pleasure,
Lying wide to three hundred in one heat,
Loving none truly, but leaving them every one
    Wrung out and dropping;

But as for my love, let her not count on it
As once she could: by her own fault it died
As a flower at the edge of a field, which the plow
    Roots out in passing.

SUMMER

Be of this brightness dyed
Whose unrecking fever
Flings gold before it goes
Into voids finally
That have no measure.

Bird-sleep, moon-set,
Island after island,
Be of their hush
On this tide that balance
A time, for a time.

Islands are not forever,
Nor this light again,
Tide-set, brief summer,
Be of their secret
That fears no other.

SOME WINTER SPARROWS

i

I hear you already, choir of small wheels,
    Through frayed trees I see your
Shaken flight like a shiver
Of thin light on a river.

ii

On a bitter day I juggle feathers,
    My hands hatch, I am better
Answered than puppet masters,
With small winds at my fingers.

iii

You pursue seeds, wings open on the snow,
    Coming up then with white
Beak, speaking; in my deep foot-prints
You vanish, then you flower.

iv

Like no other: one white feather in either
    Wing, every turn of yours
Surprises me; you are quicker,
Girl, than the catch in my breath.

v

Vanity: alone with many crumbs, teasing
    Each briefly. When the rest

Get here, the crumb nearest you
Will be worth scrapping over.

vi

Caught in flight by harbor winds, you stumble
  In air, your strung-out flock
Shudders sideways, sinking, like
A net when heavy fish strike.

vii

More snow: under a green fir-bush bowed low
  With flakes broad as cats' paws
You hunch, puffed: if you do not
Move maybe it will go away.

viii

I find you too late, shrivelled lid half drawn,
  Grimy eye, your wings' rigor,
Dishevelled breast feathers worse
Than ice inside my closed hand.

ix

And more than one. Who would save bits of string
  Kinked as stubbornly, as short,
As dirty, knotted together
Into fours, as your feet are?

x

You shriek like nails on a slate, one of you
  Falls dead at my feet, skull
Split; and it is still winter,
Not yet the season for love.

xi

Those blue pigeons: there is snow still to fall,
But in the brief sun they
Bob, gobble, begin their dance.
You doze then, row of old men.

xii

Whether the gray cat is at the corner,
The hawk hunting over
The graves, or the light too late
To trust, you will not come down.

PLEA FOR A CAPTIVE

Woman with the caught fox
By the scruff, you can drop your hopes:
It will not tame though you prove kind,
Though you entice it with fat ducks
Patiently to your fingertips
And in dulcet love enclose it
Do not suppose it will turn friend,
Dog your heels, sleep at your feet,
Be happy in the house,
                              No,

It will only trot to and fro,
To and fro, with vacant eye,
Neither will its pelt improve
Nor its disposition, twisting
The raw song of its debasement
Through the long nights, and in your love,
In your delicate meats tasting
Nothing but its own decay
(As at first hand I have learned)
                              Oh

Kill it at once or let it go.

CHOICE OF PRIDES

for Dido

To tell the truth, it would have its points
(Since fall we must) to do it proud:
To ride for your fall on a good mount
Hung with honors and looped garlands,
Moved by the crowd's flattering sounds,
Or to advance with brash din, banners,
Flights of arrows leaping like hounds.

But from a choice of prides I would pick
(Or so I hope) the bare cheek
To amble out, innocent of arms
And alone, under the cocked guns
Or what missiles might be in season,
And this in the pure brass of the act
Attired, and in no other armor.

Considering that, of every species
(I should reason) mine is most naked,
For all its draperies enacting
As a pink beast its honest nature,
I will take in this raw condition
What pride I can, not have my boast
In glad-rags, my bravery plated.

And I should think myself twice lucky
(Stuck with my choice) if I could be sure
That I had been egged on by nothing

But neat pride, and not (as is common,)
Brought to it by the veiled promptings
Of vanity, or by poverty
Or the fecklessness of despair.

THE CLIMB

Where, like a whip, at the foot of the stairs
The banister rail licks round at them,
In a hushed flock they find they are huddled:
The night defunct, in their upturned faces
The party gone out like a light,
And more than one of them open-mouthed
As horses reined up suddenly,
                    Hearing
Above the blood drumming in their ears
And the crepitant bulb in the dumb house,
Strained banisters creaking like rockers
Where the lurching cripple, drunk as a kite,
Scrapes, thuds, and snuffling half the time
On all fours, hauls himself upwards
On the stairs over their heads,
                    Like
Some weakness of their own: not to be helped
(Rather turn offensive) and at no time
To be denied—inviting himself
Along with them on the wrong occasion
That way, and soon goatish in his liquor,
Stumbling in boats by the moonlit lake,
Clawing and hugging not to fall—
                    Ground out
From under his scuffling and skew stumps,
The racketing music of his ascent
Rains down on their faces, like stones dropped
Into a well, and it will echo,
Discordant, among them long after

They have heard him reach his room finally
And heard the door shut on their shame.

BLIND GIRL

Silent, with her eyes
Climbing above her like a pair of hands drowning,
Up the tower stairs she runs headlong, turning
In a spiral of voices that grow no fainter, though
At each turn, through the tiny window,
The blood-shrieking starlings, flaking into the trees,
Sound farther below.

Still, as she runs
Turn above turn round the hollow flights, so
Ringing higher, the towering voices follow,
Out of each room renewed as she passes,
To echo, hopeless: their shrieked entreaties
Singing their love, and their gross resonance
Her beauty's praises,

With no name too tender,
High, or childish to din their desperate
Invocations; confessing; swearing to dedicate
Their split hearts on salvers if only she
Will pause. Each raw plea raucous less to delay,
At last, than to claim her: "Though you turn for no other,
Dear soul, this is me, me!"

But buffeted and stunned
By their spun cries as in clambering water,
Now if she tried she could not remember
Which door among those, nor what care, crime,
Possession, name, she had bolted from,

Nor how, the way opening to her blind hand,
    She had slipped past them,

    Nor how many centuries
Ago. Only tells herself over and over
That their winding calls cannot forever
Build, but at their shrill peak stairs, tower, all
Into the loose air sprung suddenly, will fall,
Breathless, to nothing, and instantly her repose
    Be silent and final.

ONE-EYE

("In the country of the blind the one-eyed man is king.")

On that vacant day
After kicking and moseying here and there
For some time, he lifted that carpet-corner
    His one eye-lid, and the dyed light
Leapt at him from all sides like dogs. Also hues
That he had never heard of, in that place
    Were bleeding and playing.

Even so, it was
Only at the grazing of light fingers
Over his face, unannounced, and then his
    Sight of many mat eyes, paired white
Irises like dried peas looking, that it dawned
On him: his sidelong idling had found
    The country of the blind.

Whose swarming digits
Knew him at once: their king, come to them
Out of a saying. And chanting an anthem
    Unto his one eye, to the dry
Accompaniment that their leaping fingers made
Flicking round him like locusts in a cloud,
    They took him home with them.

Their shapely city
Shines like a suit. On a plain chair he was set
In a cloak of hands, and crowned, to intricate
    Music. They sent him their softest

Daughters, clad only in scent and their own
Vast ears, meantime making different noises
      In each ante-chamber.

            They can be wakened
Sometimes by a feather falling on the next
Floor, and they keep time by the water-clocks'
      Dropping even when they sleep. Once
He would expound to them all, from his only
Light, day breaking, the sky spiked and the
      Earth amuck with color,

            And they would listen,
Amazed at his royalty, gaping like
Sockets, and would agree, agree, blank
      As pearls. At the beginning.
Alone in brightness, soon he spoke of it
In sleep only; "Look, look," he would call out
      In the dark only.

            Now in summer gaudy
With birds he says nothing; of their thefts, often
Beheld, and their beauties, now for a long time
      Nothing. Nothing, day after day,
To see the black thumb as big as a valley
Over their heads descending silently
      Out of a quiet sky.

SMALL WOMAN ON SWALLOW STREET

Four feet up, under the bruise-blue
Fingered hat-felt, the eyes begin. The sly brim
Slips over the sky, street after street, and nobody
Knows, to stop it. It will cover
The whole world, if there is time. Fifty years'
Start in gray the eyes have; you will never
Catch up to where they are, too clever
And always walking, the legs not long but
The boots big with wide smiles of darkness
Going round and round at their tops, climbing.
They are almost to the knees already, where
There should have been ankles to stop them.
So must keep walking all the time, hurry, for
The black sea is down where the toes are
And swallows and swallows all. A big coat
Can help save you. But eyes push you down; never
Meet eyes. There are hands in hands, and love
Follows its furs into shut doors; who
Shall be killed first? Do not look up there:
The wind is blowing the building-tops, and a hand
Is sneaking the whole sky another way, but
It will not escape. Do not look up. God is
On High. He can see you. You will die.

THE GLEANERS

They always gather on summer nights there
On the corner under the buggy street-bulb,
Chewing their dead stubs outside the peeling
    Bar, those foreign old men,

Till the last street-car has squealed and gone
An hour since into the growing silence,
Leaving only the bugs' sounds, and their own breathing;
    Sometime then they hobble off.

Some were already where they stay, last night,
In rooms, fumbling absently with laces,
Straps, trusses, one hand was nearly to a glass
    With a faceful of teeth

At the time the siren went shrieking for
The fire in the cigar factory there,
Half the town by then stinking like a crooked
    Stogie. Well there they are

Where all day they have been, beetling over
The charred pile, teetering like snails and careful
Under sooty hats, in ankle shoes, vests,
    Shirts grimed at collars and wrists,

Bending, babying peck baskets as they
Revolve on painful feet over the rubble,
Raking with crooked knuckles the amber pools
    For limp cheroots.

After dark there will still be a few turning
Slowly with flashlights. Except for coughs they are quiet;
Sober; they always knew something would happen,
    Something would provide.

POOL ROOM IN THE LIONS' CLUB

I'm sure it must be still the same,
Year after year, the faded room
Upstairs out of the afternoon,
The spidery hands, stalking and cautious
Round and round the airless light,
The few words like the dust settling
Across the quiet, the shadows waiting
Intent and still around the table
For the ivory click, the sleeves stirring,
Swirling the smoke, the hats circling
Remote and hazy above the light,
The board creaking, then hushed again.
Trains from the sea-board rattle past,
And from St. Louis and points west,
But nothing changes their concern,
Hurries or calls them. They must think
The whole world is nothing more
Than their gainless harmless pastime
Of utter patience protectively
Absorbed around one smooth table
Safe in its ring of dusty light
Where the real dark can never come.

JOHN OTTO

John Otto of Brunswick, ancestor
On my mother's side, Latin scholar,
Settler of the Cumberland Valley,
Schoolmaster, sire of a family,
Why, one day in your white age,
Did you heave up onto your old man's legs
In the house near Blain, in Perry County,
And shut the gate and shuffle away
From the home of eighty years or so
And what cronies were left, and follow
The road out of the valley, up the hill,
Over the south mountain, to Carlisle,
The whole way on foot, in the wagon tracks,
To die of fatigue there, at ninety-six?
I can see Carlisle Valley spread below
And you, John, coming over the hill's brow,
Stopping for breath and a long look;
I can hear your breath come sharp and quick,
But why it was that you climbed up there
None of us remembers any more.
To see your son and his family?
Was the house too quiet in Perry County?
To ask some question, tell some secret,
Or beg some pardon before too late?
Or was it to look once again
On another valley green in the sun
Almost as in the beginning, to remind
Your eyes of a promise in the land?

UNCLE HESS

Wriest of uncles, and most remote, Sam Hess,
Who named your tall daughter for the goddess
Minerva, whom all agreed she resembled
Till her car smashed with her and Olympus crumbled,
You had had enough of deities by then—
With neither of you as young as you had been,
And she some years a widow—for gods had proved
As mortal as anything that could be loved,
And loveable only as they seemed human.
Folks said they'd know that walk of yours in Japan,
But not what you would do next, who provided
A thermometer for the chicken shed
So the hens, if they chose, could read how hot
In the tin shade the latter day had got
And comfort themselves with knowledge. Whereas you deigned
To recognize your family, in the end,
Only on certain days when the air was right,
You were always, while not approachable, polite,
And wore your Panama till the hour you died,
For the mad world must be kept mystified
Or it would bite. Canny and neat, whatever
You were was unmistakable, but never
Could be explained. And I wonder whether
Even now you would tell me anything more
Of every kinship than its madness,
If I could ask you, here, under your trees,
By your big house that watches the river still
Turning the cranky wheels of your mill
Before it twists toward Ohio around the bend
As though there were no questions and no end.

GRANDFATHER IN THE OLD MEN'S HOME

Gentle at last, and as clean as ever,
He did not even need drink any more,
And his good sons unbent and brought him
Tobacco to chew, both times when they came
To be satisfied he was well cared for.
And he smiled all the time to remember
Grandmother, his wife, wearing the true faith
Like an iron nightgown, yet brought to birth
Seven times and raising the family
Through her needle's eye while he got away
Down the green river, finding directions
For boats. And himself coming home sometimes
Well-heeled but blind drunk, to hide all the bread
And shoot holes in the bucket while he made
His daughters pump. Still smiled as kindly in
His sleep beside the other clean old men
To see Grandmother, every night the same,
Huge in her age, with her thumbed-down mouth, come
Hating the river, filling with her stare
His gliding dream, while he turned to water,
While the children they both had begotten,
With old faces now, but themselves shrunken
To child-size again, stood ranged at her side,
Beating their little Bibles till he died.

GRANDMOTHER WATCHING AT
HER WINDOW

There was always the river or the train
Right past the door, and someone might be gone
Come morning. When I was a child I mind
Being held up at a gate to wave
Good-bye, good-bye to I didn't know who,
Gone to the War, and how I cried after.
When I married I did what was right
But I knew even that first night
That he would go. And so shut my soul tight
Behind my mouth, so he could not steal it
When he went. I brought the children up clean
With my needle, taught them that stealing
Is the worst sin; knew if I loved them
They would be taken away, and did my best
But must have loved them anyway
For they slipped through my fingers like stitches.
Because God loves us always, whatever
We do. You can sit all your life in churches
And teach your hands to clutch when you pray
And never weaken, but God loves you so dearly
Just as you are, that nothing you are can stay,
But all the time you keep going away, away.

GRANDMOTHER DYING

Not ridden in her Christian bed, either,
But her wrenched back bent double, hunched over
The plank tied to the arms of her rocker
With a pillow on it to keep her head
Sideways up from her knees, and three others
Behind her in the high chair to hold her
Down so the crooked might be straight, as if
There was any hope. Who for ninety-three years,
Keeping the faith, believed you could get
Through the strait gate and the needle's eye if
You made up your mind straight and narrow, kept
The thread tight and, dead both to left and to right
To the sly music beyond the ditches, beat
Time on the book as you went. And then she fell.
She should have did what she was told, she should
Have called for what she needed, she did look
Sleeping on the pillows and to be trusted
Just for a bit, and Bid was not downstairs
A minute before hearing the hall creak
And the door crash back in the bathroom as
She fell. What was it, eighteen months, they took
Care of her crooked that way, feeding from
The side, hunching down to hear her, all
Knowing full well what the crooked come to
When their rockers stop. Still could hear what she
Thought good to hear, still croak: you keep my
Candy hid in that sweater drawer, Bid,
Only for company one piece, then you put it
Back again, hear? One after the other
A family of fevers visited her,

And last a daughter-in-law with a nasty
Cough combed her hair out pretty on the plank,
With a flower in it, and held a mirror
For her to see till it made her smile, but
Bid, she whispered, you keep wide of that new
Nurse's cough, she has T.B. And where
Were the wars that still worried her, when
Most were dead a long time ago, and one
Son had come back and was there hanging
In sunlight, in a medal of glory, on
The wall in her room smelling of coal-gas
And petunias. One daughter lived and dusted
A nice brick house a block away, already
Rehearsing how she'd say, "Well, we was always
Good to our Mumma anyway." Outside,
The crooked river flowed easy, knowing
All along; the tracks smiled and rang away;
Help would come from the hills. One knotted hand
Of hers would hang up in the air above
Her head for hours, propped on its elbow, waving
In that direction. And when she heaved up
Her last breath, to shake it like a fist,
As out of a habit so old as to be
Nearly absent, at the dirty river
Sliding away there the same as ever,
Bid says you could not hear her because there
Came a black engine that had been waiting
Up the tracks there for ninety-four years, and
Snatched it out from her lips, and roared off
With it hooting downriver, making the tracks
Straighten out in front of it like a whip,
While the windows rattled loud to break, the things
On the shelves shook, the folds of her face jarred
And shivered; and when it was gone, for a long
Time the goosed laundry still leaped and jiggled
In the smutty wind outside, and her chair went on

Rocking all by itself with nothing alive
Inside it to explain it, nothing, nothing.

THE NATIVE

for Agatha and Stephen Fassett

He and his, unwashed all winter,
In that abandoned land in the punished
North, in a gnashing house sunk as a cheek,
Nest together, a bunting bundle crumpled
Like a handkerchief on the croaking
Back-broken bed jacked up in the kitchen; the clock
Soon stops, they just keep the cooker going; all
Kin to begin with when they crawl in under,
      Who covers who they don't care.

He and his, in the settled cozy,
Steam like a kettle, rock-a-bye, the best
Went west long ago, got out from under,
Waved bye-bye to the steep scratched fields and scabby
Pastures: their chapped plaster of newspapers
Still chafes from the walls, and snags of string tattling
Of their rugs trail yet from stair-nails. The rest,
Never the loftiest, left to themselves,
      Descended, descended.

Most that's his, at the best of times,
Looks about to fall: the propped porch lurches
Through a herd of licked machines crutched in their last
Seizures, each as ominously leaning
As the framed ancestors, trapped in their collars,
Beetling out of oval clouds from the black
Tops of the rooms, their unappeasable jowls

By nothing but frayed, faded cords leashed
                To the leaking walls.

                But they no more crash
Onto him and his than the cobwebs, or
The gritting rafters, though on the summer-people's
Solid houses the new-nailed shingles open
All over like doors, flap, decamp, the locked
Shutters peel wide to wag like clappers
At the clattering windows, and the cold chimneys
Scatter bricks downwind, like the smoking heads
                Of dandelions.

                In his threadbare barn, through
The roof like a snag-toothed graveyard the snow
Cradles and dives onto the pitched backs
Of his cow and plowhorse each thin as hanging
Laundry, and it drifts deep on their spines
So that one beast or other, almost every winter
Lets its knees stiffly down and freezes hard
To the barn floor; but his summer employers
                Always buy him others.

                For there is no one else
Handy in summer, there in winter,
And he and his can dream at pleasure,
It is said, of houses burning, and do so
All through the cold, till the spooled snakes sleeping under
The stone dairy-floor stir with the turned year,
Waken, and sliding loose in their winter skins
Like air rising through thin ice, feed themselves forth
                To inherit the earth.

BURNING MOUNTAIN

No blacker than others in winter, but
The hushed snow never arrives on that slope.
An emanation of steam on damp days,
With a faint hiss, if you listen some places,
Yes, and if you pause to notice, an odor,
Even so near the chimneyed city, these
Betray what the mountain has at heart. And all night,
Here and there, popping in and out of their holes
Like ground-hogs gone nocturnal, the shy flames.

Unnatural, but no mystery.
Many are still alive to testify
Of the miner who left his lamp hanging
Lit in the shaft and took the lift, and never
Missed a thing till, half-way home to supper
The bells' clangor caught him. He was the last
You'd have expected such a thing from;
The worrying kind, whose old-womanish
Precautions had been a joke for years.

Smothered and silent, for some miles the fire
Still riddles the fissured hill, deviously
Wasting and inextinguishable. They
Have sealed off all the veins they could find,
Thus at least setting limits to it, we trust.
It consumes itself, but so slowly it will outlast
Our time and our grandchildren's, curious
But not unique: there was always one of these
Nearby, wherever we moved, when I was a child.

Under it, not far, the molten core
Of the earth recedes from its thin crust
Which all the fires we light cannot prevent
From cooling. Not a good day's walk above it
The meteors burn out in the air to fall
Harmless in empty fields, if at all.
Before long it practically seemed normal,
With its farms on it, and wells of good water,
Still cold, that should last us, and our grandchildren.

GRANDMOTHER AND GRANDSON

As I hear it, now when there is company
Always the spindly granddam, stuck standing
In her corner like a lady clock long
Silent, out of some hole in the talk
Is apt to clack cup, clatter teeth, and with
Saucer gesturing to no one special,
Shake out her paper voice concerning
That pimply boy her last grandson: "Now who,
Who does he remind you of?

                (Who stuffs there
With cake his puffed face complected half
Of yellow crumbs, his tongue loving over
His damp hands to lick the sticky
From bitten fingers; chinless; all boneless but
His neck and knees; and who now rolls his knowing
Eyes to their attention.)

            In vain, in vain,
One after the other, their lusterless
Suggestions of faint likenesses; she
Nods at none, her gaze absent and more
Absent, as though watching for someone through
A frosted window, until they are aware
She has forgotten her own question.

When he is alone, though, with only her
And her hazy eyes in the whole house
To mind him, his way is to take himself
Just out of her small sight and there stay

Till she starts calling; let her call till she
Sounds in pain; and as though in pain, at last,
His answers, each farther, leading her
Down passages, up stairs, with her worry
Hard to swallow as a scarf-end, her pace
A spun child's in a blindfold, to the piled
Dust-coop, trunk- and junk-room at the top
Of all the stairs, where he hides till she sways
Clutching her breath in the very room, then
Behind her slips out, locking the door. His
Laughter down stair after stair she hears
Being forgotten. In the unwashed light,
Lost, she turns among the sheeted mounds
Fingering hems and murmuring, "Where, where
Does it remind me of?" Till someone comes.

THE HOTEL-KEEPERS

All that would meet
The eyes of the hawks who slid southward
Like paired hands, year after year,
Over the ridge bloody with autumn
Would be the two iron roofs,
House and barn, high in the gap huddled,
Smoke leaking from the stone stack,
A hotel sign from one hook dangling,
And the vacant wagon-track
Trailing across the hog-backed mountain
With no other shack in sight
For miles. So an ignorant stranger
Might rein up there as night fell
(Though warned by his tired horse's rearing
At nothing near the barn door)
And stopping, never be seen after;
Thus pedlars' wares would turn up
Here and there minus their lost pedlars;
Hounds nosing over the slope
Far downwind would give tongue suddenly
High and frantic, closing in
On the back door; and in the valley
Children raucous as starlings
Would start behaving at the mention
Of the Hotel-Man.

Who was not tall,
Who stumped slowly, brawny in gum-boots,
And who spoke little, they said
(Quarrymen, farmers, all the local

Know-it-alls). Who was seen once,
When a nosey passer-by followed
    Low noises he thought were moans,
Standing with raised axe in the hayloft,
    And whose threats that time, although
Not loud, pursued the rash intruder
    For months. But who, even so,
Holed up in his squat house, five decades
    Outwintered the righteous wrath
And brute schemes they nursed in the valley,
    Accidents, as they well knew,
Siding with him, and no evidence
    With them. And survived to sit,
Crumpled with age, and be visited
    Blabbing in his swivel-chair
With eyes adrift and wits dismantled,
    From sagging lip letting fall
Allusions of so little judgment
    That his hotel doors at last
Were chained up and all callers fielded
    By his anxious wife.

        A pleasant soul
Herself, they agreed: her plump features
    Vacant of malice, her eyes
Hard to abhor. And once he was crated
    And to his patient grave shrugged
(Where a weedy honor over him
    Seeded itself in no time)
They were soon fetching out their soft hearts
    To compare, calling to mind
Sickness, ruffians, the mountain winter,
    Her solitude, her sore feet,
Haling her down with all but music,
    Finally, to the valley,
To stand with bared gums, to be embraced,
    To be fussed over, dressed up

In their presents, and with kind people
     Be settled in a good house,
To turn chatty, to be astonished
     At nothing, to sit for hours
At her window facing the mountain,
     Troubled by recollections
No more than its own loosening stream
     Cracking like church pews, in spring,
Or the hawks, in fall, sailing over
     To their own rewards.

THE DRUNK IN THE FURNACE

For a good decade
The furnace stood in the naked gully, fireless
And vacant as any hat. Then when it was
No more to them than a hulking black fossil
To erode unnoticed with the rest of the junk-hill
By the poisonous creek, and rapidly to be added
          To their ignorance,

          They were afterwards astonished
To confirm, one morning, a twist of smoke like a pale
Resurrection, staggering out of its chewed hole,
And to remark then other tokens that someone,
Cosily bolted behind the eye-holed iron
Door of the drafty burner, had there established
          His bad castle.

          Where he gets his spirits
It's a mystery. But the stuff keeps him musical:
Hammer-and-anvilling with poker and bottle
To his jugged bellowings, till the last groaning clang
As he collapses onto the rioting
Springs of a litter of car-seats ranged on the grates,
          To sleep like an iron pig.

          In their tar-paper church
On a text about stoke-holes that are sated never
Their Reverend lingers. They nod and hate trespassers.
When the furnace wakes, though, all afternoon
Their witless offspring flock like piped rats to its siren
Crescendo, and agape on the crumbling ridge
          Stand in a row and learn.

W. S. MERWIN

W. S. Merwin was born in New York City in 1927 and grew up in
Union City, New Jersey, and in Scranton, Pennsylvania. From 1949 to
1951 he worked as a tutor in France, Portugal, and Majorca. After that,
for several years he made the greater part of his living by translating
from French, Spanish, Latin and Portuguese. Since 1954 several
fellowships have been of great assistance. In addition to poetry, he has
written articles, chiefly for *The Nation*, and radio scripts for the BBC.
He has lived in England, France, and the United States. His books of
poetry are *A Mask for Janus* (1952), *The Dancing Bears* (1954), *Green
with Beasts* (1956), *The Drunk in the Furnace* (1960), *The Moving Target*
(1963), *The Lice* (1967), *The Carrier of Ladders* (1970) for which he
received the Pulitzer Prize and *Writings to an Unfinished Accompaniment*
(1973). His translations include *The Poem of the Cid* (1959), *Spanish
Ballads* (1960), *The Satires of Persius* (1961), *Lazarillo de Tormes* (1962),
The Song of Roland (1963), *Selected Translations 1948–1968* (1968), for
which he won the P.E.N. Translation Prize for 1968, *Transparence of the
World*, a translation of his selection of poems by Jean Follain (1969) and
(with Clarence Brown) *Osip Mandelstam, Selected Poems* (1974). A book
of prose, *The Miner's Pale Children*, was published in 1970. In 1974 he
was awarded The Fellowship of the Academy of American Poets.